Vyāsa Redux

Also by the same author:

The Sanskrit Hero (2004)
Strī (2009)
Jaya (2011)
Supernature (2012)
Heroic Kṛṣṇa (2013)
Eroica (2013)
In the Kacch (2015)
Windward (2015)
Arjuna Pāṇḍava (2016)
Eros (2016)
Rāja Yudhiṣṭhira (2017)
Bhīṣma Devavrata (2018)

Vyāsa Redux

Narrative in Epic Mahābhārata

Kevin McGrath

ANTHEM PRESS

Anthem Press
An imprint of Wimbledon Publishing Company
www.anthempress.com

This edition first published in UK and USA 2020
by ANTHEM PRESS
75–76 Blackfriars Road, London SE1 8HA, UK
or PO Box 9779, London SW19 7ZG, UK
and
244 Madison Ave #116, New York, NY 10016, USA

First published in the UK and USA by Anthem Press 2019

Cover image courtesy of Maximilien Guy McGrath.

British Library Cataloguing-in-Publication Data
A catalogue record for this book is available from the British Library.

ISBN-13: 978-1-78527-574-6 (Pbk)
ISBN-10: 1-78527-574-7 (Pbk)

This title is also available as an e-book.

To Robert P. Goldman
with admiration
gṛhāṇemāṃ mayā proktāṃ siddhiṃ mūrtimatīm iva
III,37,27

CONTENTS

ACKNOWLEDGEMENTS

THIS book builds upon concepts and methods that have been developed in my previous works; there my process of analysis has always been founded upon the inferences derived by a strictly empirical *explication de texte*. All of the friends and colleagues named below have either assisted or influenced my assembly of data and the subsequent formulation of inferences upon which the argumentation of this book has been founded.

I am profoundly grateful to my friends and colleagues in the Harvard Mahābhārata Seminar for all the discussion and readings that we have exchanged for more than two decades, and also to Gregory Nagy, with whom I have shared many happy hours of conversation and classroom time.

I am also deeply grateful to the generosity and kindness of Leila Ahmed, Sunil Amrith, Dorothy Austin, Homi Bhabha, Amarananda Bhairavan, Pradip Bhattacharya, Sugata Bose, Aldo Bottino, Thomas Burke, Gurcharan Das, Olga Davidson, Richard Delacy, Casey Dué, Diana Eck, David Elmer, Douglas Frame, Robert Goldman, Charles Hallisey, Lilian Handlin, Alf Hiltebeitel, Krutarthsinhji Jadeja, Stephanie Jamison, His Highness Jayasinhji I, Zulfiqar Ali Kalhoro, Leonard van der Kuijp, T. J. Markey, Daniel Mason, Leanna McGrath, Anne Monius, Susan Moore, Leonard Muellner, Abi Pandey, Parimal Patil, His Highness Pragmulji III, Howard Resnick, Amartya Sen, L. D. Shah, Oktor Skjærvø, Romila Thapar, Richard Thomas, Pulin Vasa, W. C. Weitzel and Michael Witzel.

Cambridge, 2018

Chapter 1

INTRODUCTION

Kṛṣṇa Dvaipāyana Pārāśara, known as Vyāsa, is conceived of by the makers of Epic *Mahābhārata* as the principal poet of the work, one who envisions *both* the events and then the poetic practice itself which represents those events; in this he is not only the inventor but is himself an active character within the narrative of the poem, which is paradoxical and introduces an unreasonable dimension to the epic. As such a figure, he possesses both foresight and aftersight in that he comprehends the aetiology of incidents and also apprehends their future direction.

This double activity is essentially irrational, and yet it is this irreducibly various quality of the person of Vyāsa as both composer and actor which makes the epic cohere as it does for us today. This is facilitated firstly by the presence of his *factotum*, the rhapsodic poet Vaiśaṃpāyana who performs most of the poem as we know it in the modern version of the Pune Critical Edition (PCE).[1] Then secondly, there is also another voice, that of the *sūta* Saṃjaya, who presents the central drama of the epic; he is the poet who receives his visionary inspiration directly from Vyāsa's gracious ingenuity.

This book offers an examination and analysis of the super-complex and tripartite narrative order that is primarily generated by this poet, character and *ṛṣi* or 'patriarchal seer'.[2]

As an individual, the figure of Vaiśaṃpāyana is a blank, for the audience hear and know nothing about his person or nature – he is simply a voice who

1 All *Mahābhārata* references in this book are to the PCE; on some specified occasions I also draw upon the Bombay Edition (BE) with its appended commentary of the *paṇḍita* Nīlakaṇṭha. I have also used the Purāṇic Encyclopaedia of Vettam Mani, the *Index to the Names in the Mahābhārata* of Sörensen and the online Sanskrit text of the poem during the course of this research.

2 My colleague, Susan Moore, writes about this noun as it derives from the verbal root √*ṛṣ*, 'to flow, flow quickly, glide': 'What comes to mind is the process of cognition with the *ṛṣi* acting as a conduit through which the hymns of primordial nature and creation – the Vedas – can easily flow and manifest, not unlike the process of poetry for a poet. The *ṛṣi* is the pure, uninvolved agent of manifestation for expressions of the deities and can even be construed as their ultimate source.' Personal communication, August 2018.

reports or recites what he has learned; this is unlike Saṃjaya and Vyāsa who are actually dramatic individuals in the poem as well as creative poets of the work. Vaiśaṃpāyana is like Bhīṣma, the most ancient of the heroes, who is similarly without any dramatic persona during the narration of the Śānti and Anuśāsana *parvans*, or 'books'. Ugraśravas, the voice who delivers the complete vessel or frame of the poem, is similarly lacking in any narrative personality.[3] Thus Vyāsa – unlike Vaiśaṃpāyana, Ugraśravas and the later Bhīṣma – is a figure of compound and theatrical magnitude as he and Saṃjaya are the only two poets who are dynamic and impressionable characters who both create the words and then act as personae within their working of those words.

To advance this model, in the folklore and mythology of contemporary India, Vyāsa is considered to be the actual author of the epic poem, that is, he is said to have *written* the text entirely, working with his *amanuensis* Gaṇeśa, the elephantine son of Rudra-Śiva. This fits with a standard of belief that is inherently Hindu and popular and is distinct from the more scholarly view whereby the *Great Bhārata* first developed during a period of preliteracy throughout the early first millennium BCE, drawing upon many modes of tradition, some of which were extremely archaic and deriving from regions and cultures that were beyond the borders of the subcontinent.[4]

It is this latter conception of the poem which the present book addresses, and in this I have paid especial attention not so much to the life cycle of Vyāsa but also to the nature of his influence in how the narrative of the poem has been formulated.[5] To say, however, that some of those influences originate from outside the frontiers of what we now know as India or Bhārat is often to invite political contention in the modern world.

Narrative can be described as a verbal or visual system that is sequential, either in a causally related or a temporal series. It is fundamentally a movement of metonymy – or meaning that is generated by connection – which causes an understanding of *montage*: an arrangement of images or events that appear

3 The *ṛṣi* Bhṛgu, who renders the voice that declaims the Mānava *dharmaśāstra*, is similarly without any personal identity and is merely the nominal medium of proclamation; he is someone who lacks all dramatic presence or identity, like Vaiśaṃpāyana or Ugraśravas.

4 By the term 'archaic' I refer to a society that is both preliterate and premonetary in culture; by the term 'classical' I understand a society whose culture is literate and whose economy in primarily monetary in practice. I think of the archaic as using bronze or copper alloy for their metal tools or weapons and of the classical as employing primarily iron for their implements. This is a general and essentially hermeneutic distinction, for the presence of bronze metallurgy in first-millennium northern India remains much disputed and unresolved. See Agrawal, 1971; and Coningham and Young, 2015.

5 Sullivan, 1999, has an excellent evaluative study of the life events and ritual nature of Vyāsa.

to be serially associated, thus constituting a narrative. The unique quality of *homo narrans*, unlike other creatures on this planet, is that he or she can develop narratives that are fictional and yet which are capable of conveying cultural and personal truth for their audience.

Obversely, the human brain is such that its cognitive procedures will always seek to identify narrative in any succession of images or literal scenes or even sounds.[6] To take this one step further, narrative itself can be considered as metaphorical, as with the journey and voyage of the Homeric hero Odysseus, where the poets are explicitly illustrating their view of human *nóos*, or 'consciousness', and representing how the psyche is composed and functions according to the way in which the narrative is formulated. In that case, narrative is a *facsimile* of consciousness; we shall return to the epitome of Odysseus at the end of this book.[7]

Thus the medium of narrative can bear a certain metaphorical truth for this kind of *genre* of communication – in this instant the epic poem – one that is not solely dependent upon the contents of the work but which also derives significance from its structure. This means that the multitudinous and polytropic quality of the *Great Bhārata* itself communicates its own especial and ultimate consequence, for the varying levels of metaphor depend upon who is delivering the poem at any specific moment. I shall argue that this movement of expression is essentially located upon and within the place and character of Vyāsa Pārāśara, for, as we noted above, Vyāsa is both the ideal causative agent of the original narration of the poem and also a thoroughly expressive character *within* that poem's manifestation. Vyāsa is thus a super-faceted figure, for his creativity and the production of his character occur on many coincident and sometimes paradoxical levels. Likewise, human consciousness is not simply linear and uniform but is also polytropic and multitudinous, operating from many perspectives simultaneously.

Additionally, as we have already observed, the *Great Bhārata* is founded on narrative themes and figures whose existence sometimes precedes the *idealized* production of the *Great Bhārata* itself, as evinced by similarities and identities that can be observed in other Āryan epic traditions, especially in archaic Homeric poetry. These too fall within the domain of Vyāsa's poetry.

---

6 I would strongly assert that human cognition is the source of narrative awareness and that narrative is not an objective phenomenon. One might argue that time is an empirical narration, yet time – as the cycle of the year, which is its primary form – only reiterates and repeats itself. Narration occurs *within* that temporal frame and is the human cognitive apprehension of how sensible perception can be organized.

7 The same is true of the narratives which tell of the heroes Heracles and Jason.

This study examines four essential aspects of the intellectually mobile Vyāsa, and these are developed progressively as the book advances.

The first concerns Vyāsa as the hypothetical primary composer, the initial poet who proclaimed the original *Bhārata* which later became augmented into what we presently understand as the *Great Bhārata*.

Secondly, there is a gathering of diverse poetic and sometimes political traditions which the poets drew upon during the late Bronze Age as they envisioned and composed their work. These narrative elements are vital threads within which the figure of Vyāsa was woven, for this is a poem that was in part founded upon much earlier poetic customs, characters, legends and, perhaps, terrain.

Then, thirdly, integral to such *mythemes* and developing that view of the work, there is the character of the inexhaustible Vyāsa himself, who plays a highly individual and omniscient role actually inside the drama and labour of the poem, speaking and behaving as if distinctly apart from that *ādi*-poet and often directing the plot with his words. It is as if William Shakespeare were to appear in the ten history plays which he wrote about the Tudor dynasty and lineage and was then to act as a particularly influential, personal and magical character in those dramas: both foretelling and recalling as the narrative developed. That is, he would be *both* author and superconscious actor, one who was able to supernaturally appear and disappear at will and to influence how the plot was advancing.

Fourthly, there are the consequences of Vyāsa's persona and speech, and there are three aspects to this. In the first place, these concern Saṃjaya the poet, who is initiated into possessing a visionary capacity which drives his performance when he delivers the central four Kurukṣetra Books. Then there is Bhīṣma, the greatest of epic warriors, who – as we shall see – is profoundly influenced by the same kind of inspiration which Vyāsa experiences when he first generates the poem. Bhīṣma has a profound effect on how the plot of the poem develops. Further, there are the instances in the poem where Vyāsa simply appears and – through speech – dictates how the work proceeds, or, he impresses how the emotional conditions of other characters in a particular scene are affected.

Thus the figure of Vyāsa is a kinetic metaphor indicating how the narrative of Epic *Mahābhārata* is formed and organized and how it progresses and expands as an integral poem. He is like a literary super-catalyst in that his personal, verbal and intellectual presence informs and activates the plot in so many varying and incidental ways.

In much of my work during the last two decades, I have developed a system of analysis for epic poetry founded upon a model that was first outlined and then advanced by the scholars Milman Parry, Albert Lord and Gregory Nagy.

Their methodology is established upon an examination of how archaic epic poetry was actually composed *during* preliterate performance, recognizing how those late Bronze Age poets employed and utilized *formulae*, including themes and motifs, and also how events of such epic work were able to be either compressed or expanded during production depending on the availability of time.[8]

What I have contributed to their methods concerns three further aspects of the model. Firstly, I have showed how epic poets were inspired either visually or acoustically, a conceptual instrument that I engage with in this present book during Chapter 2.[9] Secondly, I have demonstrated how it was that those poets worked from a cognitive or mnemonic point of view, particularly as it concerned their practical use of duality – *fugal* or *contrapuntal* arrangement – in their poetry.[10] Thirdly, I have drawn upon the conceptual distinction between what constituted *inspiration* and what constituted *edition*, a point that is connected with the ideal trajectories of plot and story, as explained in Chapter 2 of this present study.[11]

In a nutshell, all my research – including this present study – originally stems from a remarkable and seminal essay by Edward Hopkins which presented *kṣatriya* culture as uniquely depicted by Epic *Mahābhārata*.[12] As already noted, my conceptual understanding of ancient heroes is greatly drawn from the work of Nagy.[13] As for methodology, my inductive technique of close reading is modelled on the textual practice and teaching of Stephanie Jamison.[14]

Specifically, concerning this present study, in the next chapter I supply an overview to the questions which surround the presence of Kṛṣṇa Dvaipāyana and portray how the fundamental model of the poem's narrative is developed, originally by poets and then later by editors. This chapter offers three types of poetic inspiration and focuses upon the unique nature of Vyāsa's mode of creativity, one that addresses the practical distinction between what it is that constitutes *plot* and what it is that comprises the *story*.[15]

8 I would urge the interested reader to look at my 'Appendix on Epic Preliteracy', in McGrath, 2017a.
9 Also, see McGrath, 2011.
10 See McGrath, 2016.
11 I first advanced this example of thought and analysis in McGrath, 2018b.
12 Hopkins, 1888.
13 Nagy, 2006.
14 As, for instance, in Jamison, 1994, and 1997.
15 In sum, plot concerns the causal relation of events whilst story speaks of a temporal sequence of events. We shall advance this central point more completely in Chapter 2, for the application of this conceptual distinction lies at the heart of this present book.

Chapter 3 shows how there are other and earlier cognate traditions which the proto-poets who have nominated Vyāsa as their agent and representative of the *Great Bhārata*'s generation must have been familiar with and utilized in order to establish certain basic social and political conformations within the poetry. These comprise the prime elements of the present *Great Bhārata* and are the social and ideally historical vehicles of the poem that cohere within systems of economy, polity, kinship and jurisdiction.

The fourth chapter describes how it is that the persona of Vyāsa actually appears and disappears within the narrative of the epic – both before and after the great battle – as we know it today in the PCE version. That is, how Vyāsa is a *character* in the work who is distinct from the poet who was actually inspired to perform the original song which encapsulates, expresses and conveys the Pāṇḍava–Dhārtarāṣṭra feud. This chapter also addresses how the speech of the *ṛṣi* influences and at times directs the narrative itself within which he is a voluntary figure.

Chapter 5 examines how, during the course of the initial part of the Ādi *parvan*, the poets and editors represent the 'tradition' of Vyāsa as they know it and how this is rendered in several discrete ways. Chapter 6 is simply conclusive.

The final chapter offers an addendum which describes some of the narrative aspects and techniques that are at work in the Homeric Odyssey. This is a poem whose narrative, like that of the *Great Bhārata*, is ultra-compounded and super-sophisticated and is one that never simply moves from event to subsequent event. In the Homeric Odyssey, narrative is quite definitely a metaphor in itself and is not simply a medium for the plot and story of the poem. For Homeric Odysseus, meaning is supplied by sequence or metonymy, whereas for Achilles, his epic sequence does not provide meaning, for this hero is a figure who has access to only one metaphor and that is the vision which he alone possesses for his warrior song, his *kléos aphthiton* or his *kīrti*, 'fame'.

Considering Vyāsa in such a light, it is his command of metaphor which first creates the poem and, then, it is his control of metonymy during his presence *within* the epic as an actor and character which brings further meaning to the work. In this, his presence is akin to that of the deity Athena in the Odyssey.

I have introduced this Homeric supplement to the argument in order to offer conceptual contrast and counterpoint to our discussion about the *Bhārata* narrative, insofar as the examination of another and originally cognate tradition can illuminate our perception as to how Epic *Mahābhārata* itself has been composed by the poets and then, later, further arranged by editors. This final addition to the book amplifies the essential methodological conception which underlies Chapter 3, where the advantages of a comparative approach to these epic poems are first projected and discussed.

Chapter 2

OVERVIEW

Epic *Mahābhārata* in the Pune Critical Edition (PCE) begins with the following epigraph:

> I,1,1: *nārāyaṇaṃ namaskṛtya naraṃ caiva narottamam*
> *devīṃ sarasvatīṃ caiva tato jayam udīrayet*

It is the last *pada* which I would like to draw attention to, and to the words *jayam udīrayet*, 'one should proclaim the *Jaya*'.[1] In this chapter, let us examine how the epic poem is most fundamentally organized in terms of its narrative patterning and also see why it is that Vyāsa owns a presence in that modelling of the primary order of narration.

Why would the invisible master poet who proclaims all the voices in the present *Great Bhārata* – including that of Vyāsa – signal this particular term right at the outset of the work? 'Having just honoured the three divinities, then one should pronounce the *Jaya*', he says. I would like to take this word *jaya* as a name which allows us to prepare an overview of how Vyāsa – as formulated by the poets – is said to have founded his poem.

To develop this point let us draw upon three propositions: a first thesis pertaining to *jaya*; a second thesis regarding the semantic field encompassing another related key word, that is, *dhyāna*, or 'profound reflection', a term that is both vital and pivotal to the practice of Vyāsa's technique of poetic inspiration and composition; and a synthesis of these two propositions into an explanation of how the plot of the poem first becomes activated. These three arguments comprise within themselves seven discrete stages which advance the reasoning.

Addressing the first thesis, there are four other poets who participate in this epic, all of them characterized in varying degrees, who perform the poem on

---

1 An early and incunabulous version of this chapter was given as a lecture in February 2018 at the School of Oriental and African Studies in London. I am grateful to Nathan Hill who invited me to speak on that occasion and to Michael Willis who co-chaired the event; Robert Bracey introduced several significant historical interpretations to the discussion.

various platforms and what they do – each in their own particular fashion – is to recapitulate and to magnify the first singing of the *Bhārata* as it was initially declaimed at Takṣaśilā during a sacrifice sponsored by *rāja* Janamejaya.[2] All the individuals in the poem were long dead and the events fully completed when this first and hypothetical performance occurred.[3] The epic is in this sense what cinema studies refer to as a 'flashback'; that is, the totality of the narrative is completely analeptic.

Jaya means 'victory', but it also has another more nominal function in that it is the title of the song that was first performed by *ṛṣi* Vyāsa on the occasion of that initial and initiating sacrifice. This is the primary and foundational speech act which first establishes the existence of the work in the sublunar world. The poets say about this proto-poem,

> I,1,61: *caturviṃśatisāhasrīṃ cakre bhāratasaṃhitām*
> He made the Bhārata composition twenty-four thousand [*ślokas*].

This is the founding *myth* of the epic, and this *ur*-poem is later said to be called *Jaya*: *jayo nameti* (I,56,19).[4] During the course of the Ādi *parvan*, however, this distinction between the *Bhārata* and *Mahābhārata* is at times imprecise and it is as if the poets are often using these words as lightly fungible synonyms.

Thus there is a certain representation of that first performance of the *Bhārata* epic and its quantitative duration is so described, yet we have no access now to whatever that earliest expression was and it remains completely suppositional, simply standing as the assumed master signifier which generates the rest of the poem we presently refer to as the *Mahābhārata*.

That initial singing therefore is somewhat akin to the zero in mathematics, for it is a value which has no ostensible practical worth and yet its use and reference facilitates all acts of further numeration. This is the primary element of the poem which cannot be retrieved, recalled or identified, and yet it implies and qualifies all other succeeding renditions of the epic as we presently know it. This would be the first thesis.

In this, the situation is similar to what nineteenth-century Hellenic classicists once considered to be the *Homeric Question*, for they struggled in their analyses

---

2 Stated at XVIII,5,29.

3 Also, let us remember that all of these poets, including Vyāsa, are actually fictions created by those who worked in the late Bronze Age tradition of the Bhārata Song.

4 In the Bombay Edition (BE) this correlation between the *Jaya* and the *Bhārata* is also made at XVIII,5,23–24. Curiously and uniquely, in this final chapter of the BE the poets distinguish between the *vācaka*, 'reciter', and the *śrotā*, 'listener' (XVIII,5,2 and 24).

to identify the parts of the Homeric corpus which possessed an archaic priority. By priority, here we understand a body of poetry which demonstrated not simply temporal antecedence but also stylistic, cultural or perhaps even geographical conditions which implied an 'earlier' phase of the poem.[5]

As a secondary point here and to advance our initial thesis, it is remarkable that in the *parvasaṃgraha*, 'the summary of books', which is given at the outset of the epic, the poets tell of how the four Kurukṣetra Books (VI–IX), plus the tenth, Sauptika *parvan*, contain a total of 23,783 verses, which is almost identical in size to the putative *ur*-poem of Vyāsa that we have just mentioned. Let us now investigate and elaborate upon this congruity between the measure of these five books and the *ideal* quantity of Vyāsa's *Bhārata* and then consider the actual poet who performs the four Kurukṣetra Books, that is, Saṃjaya.

In a study of Homeric poetics, Nagy outlined two kinds of poetry: the *aoidic* and the *rhapsodic*.[6] The former kind of poet, the *aoidos*, was one who lived and sang during archaic and preliterate times, composing his work during performance, whilst the latter figure was a type of poet who lived during a later and more classical period when literacy was extant. The *rhapsōidos* learned and recited his script, whereas the earlier model of poetry was not a fixed recitation but a spontaneous composition specific and unique to each performance: the former is learned whilst the latter is inspired. Thus an *aoidos* would produce his work anew during each performance, varying the duration of the song according to circumstances, and – like a jazz musician or a rap artist of today – he would draw upon a vast repertoire of epithets, phrases, verbal formulations, even motifs and themes, as he developed the narrative. Whereas, a *rhapsodic* poet would recite what he had previously learned, that is, he delivered a text which he had memorized verbatim.

Applying this distinction in poetic creativity to the Sanskrit epic, one observes that Saṃjaya, who sings the four Kurukṣetra Books, is inspired visually, for he is said to possess *divyaṃ cakṣur*, a supernatural gift which he receives from Vyāsa (V,129,13).[7] With this ability Saṃjaya is able to perceive events as they occur far away in the distance; he is also able to hear what is being said and, moreover, he is able to apprehend what is even being thought during those remote occasions.

Vaiśaṃpāyana, however, who delivers most of Epic *Mahābhārata*, is inspired acoustically; he himself admits that he repeats what he once heard Vyāsa declaim. He says, *pravakṣyāmi mataṃ kṛtsnaṃ vyāsasya*, 'I shall proclaim the entire

---

5 Scholars like Frame, 2009, for instance, refer to what they consider to be an early Ionian stage or dimension of the Homeric Iliad.

6 Nagy, 2003.

7 Saṃjaya himself describes this gift at VI,16,7–8.

thought of Vyāsa' (I,55,2). That is, he repeats what he has learned from his *guru* who performed at that preliminary ceremonial rite at Takṣaśilā.

I have elsewhere argued that these two epic poets are akin to the ancient Greek *aoidos* and the *rhapsōidos*.[8] I demonstrated how – according to this reasoning – Saṃjaya was the earlier kind of poet who lived and worked during preliterate times whilst Vaiśaṃpāyana was a poet who flourished during a literate and classical period. What is *seen* is, of course, antecedent to what is *heard*, and in an economic sense the *aoidic* poet actually creates value whereas the *rhapsodic* poet simply transmits value which he has received.

Now, much of Books Six to Nine are made up of verbal formulae, of similes, metaphors and phrases that with slight modulation are repeated; I would suggest that at least 80 per cent of these books are constituted by formulaic expression, for there is little actual temporal narrative in this part of the poem and it is there that the finest 'poetry' is to be discovered due to the vast proliferation of metaphor.[9] It was the *aoidic* poets who worked in this manner, employing an immense range of formulae as they composed their song. The *rhapsōidos* simply repeated the poem which he had learned and did not depend upon the necessary utility of formulaic expression, nor did he extemporize as he performed or spontaneously engage with hundreds of similes and metaphors.

Thus, in this vein of thought, the four Kurukṣetra Books, both quantitatively and stylistically, are arguably older and more primary than the rest of the poem which we presently consider to be the *Great Bhārata*. These four *parvans* are what I would assert as being the substance of the *Jaya* poem, or the initial Bhārata Song narrated by Vyāsa: our first thesis.

As a second thesis, let us now develop our argument in an opposite direction and examine how it was that Vyāsa himself became inspired; this brings us to the second of our key words, *dhyāna*. At the outset of the Bhīṣma *parvan* the poets say of him, *kavīndro [...] dhyānam anvagamat param*, 'the Indra of poets practiced high meditation' (VI,4,1). This is immediately prior to where the *sūta* Saṃjaya commences his performance and the four Kurukṣetra Books begin to appear. Thus, the inspiration of Vyāsa, the poet who is said to deliver the initial voice and expression of the *Bhārata*, is here delivered in a fashion that is completely *unlike* how the two other key poets in the epic receive their words, for it is neither visual nor audial. This kind of poetic stimulus is unique and is founded upon private or personal knowledge and not upon sensible experience.

---

8 McGrath, 2011.

9 See Vassilkov, 1995.

It is notable that where – as we have argued – the earliest or most archaic style of poetry occurs in these four central and *aoidic* books at the outset of this part of the epic, there is a unique instance which portrays the inspirational manner of Vyāsa, the supposedly first and originating poet of the *Bhārata.* It is at this coincidental point, at the opening of the Bhīṣma *parvan*, that the *Jaya* poem commences, and I would therefore assert that what became the *Great Bhārata* song is founded upon and generated by this primary act of *dhyāna* by Vyāsa which the poets here present.

This yogic ability enables him to connect with and become motivated and stimulated by the supernal system which envelops and contains the mortal or terrestrial world. Such a performance later becomes the imperishable and indestructible song of which the poets themselves declare, *nārado'śrāvayed devān [...] vedasamitam*, 'Nārada caused the deities to hear the equal-to-the Vedas', that is, Epic *Mahābhārata* (XVIII,5,42–43).

To recapitulate, the *Bhārata* has in this sense become the pattern, paradigm or template of the universe, which is first made accessible through the work of *dhyāna* and then consequently transmitted *via* the poets and ultimately back towards the deities; it is arguably this song which therefore underlies all historical or moral experience as it occurs on an earthly sublunar plateau where the poem is successively performed. That is how the epic establishes itself as *the* narrative source of dharmic awareness or consciousness for its community of ancient auditors and modern readers. To this effect, the poem repeatedly stresses how the act of *listening* to the poem being performed or to perform it oneself will have spiritual and moral effect for the audience:

> XVIII,5,53: *mahābhāratam ākhyānaṃ yaḥ paṭhet susamāhitaḥ*
> *sa gacchet paramāṃ siddhim iti me nāsti saṃśayaḥ*
> Whoever devoutly recites the Mahābhārata cycle,
> That person would go to the highest perfection, I have no doubt.

To augment this second thesis, and pursuing this idea of *dhyāna* as the primary derivation of the poem, let us now enquire where else in the epic the term appears. To my present knowledge, the word only occurs as it concerns the peculiar amity which exists between Bhīṣma and Kṛṣṇa, two leading heroes who at times communicate telepathically with each other due to their aptitude in the practice of *dhyānayoga.*

The poets say of Kṛṣṇa, *dhyānaṃ [...] anvapadyata*, 'he practiced meditation' (XII,45,20). The poets comment similarly at XII,53,2 when they say of Kṛṣṇa during predawn rites, *dhyānapatham āśritya*, 'having entered the way of meditation', then, *dadhyau brahma sanātanam*, 'he meditated on the perpetual Bráhman'.

Then, before he sets off towards Kurukṣetra with *rāja* Yudhiṣṭhira, Kṛṣṇa makes the comment about Bhīṣma that the old hero is practising this same kind of mental solicitude. He says,

XII,46,11: *māṃ dhyāti puruṣavyāgras tato me tad gataṃ manaḥ*
The man-tiger meditates on me, thus my mind has gone to that.

That is, Kṛṣṇa is indicating an instant of unique telepathic and dhyānic communication which is occurring between the two heroes at this moment in the poem.

Simultaneously and reciprocally, Bhīṣma, the old and moribund warrior, sings a hymn of praise to Kṛṣṇa beginning at XII,47,10 and continuing for 52 *ślokas*. He does this silently, communicating yogically, and the poets say that *kṛṣṇaṃ pradadhyau*, 'he meditated on Kṛṣṇa' (XII,47,7). It is not the case of *uvāca* or *abravīt*, 'he spoke' or 'he said', for nothing is being overtly declared as this is a conceptual performance on the part of the sagacious warrior; it is not audible speech but is what Bhīṣma himself refers to as *vāgyajña*, 'a sacrifice of language'. That is, the actual praising of Kṛṣṇa occurs during this practice of 'profound reflection' and is not outwardly or sensibly delivered; this praise song is incidentally dexterously and robustly monotheistic in nature. For instance, Bhīṣma says of Kṛṣṇa,

XII,47,11: *suciḥ śuciṣadaṃ haṃsaṃ tatparaḥ parameṣṭinam*
yuktvā sarvātman ātmānaṃ taṃ prapadye prajāpatim
Purity, dwelling in light, universal spirit, absolutely devoted, the superlative:
Having joined the self of all selves, I embrace that Prajāpati.

Now, to develop this point by referring back in time, I would argue that the facility of immediate and supernatural communication which occurs between these two warriors is built upon or inaugurated by an earlier incident in Book Five during a meeting which took place in the *sabhā*, 'audience hall', at Hāstinapura when Kṛṣṇa was serving as the *dūta*, 'the messenger', of *rāja* Yudhiṣṭhira.

There, an instant of theophany ensues as Kṛṣṇa exposes his divine nature to the assembled *kṣatriyas*, 'warriors', all of whom are unable to witness this and they close their eyes – that is, except for the good triumvirate of Bhīṣma,

Droṇa and Vidura. The primordial Vedic cosmos issues and emanates from Kṛṣṇa's body, much as during the Gītā theophany when all the archaic Indo-Āryan deities appeared to materialize from his mouth:

V,129,4: *aṅguṣṭhamātrās tridashā mumuchuḥ pāvakārciṣaḥ*
tasya brahmā lalāṭastho rudro vakṣasi cābhavat
lokapālā bhujeṣvāsann agnir āsyād ajāyata
ādityāś caiva sādhyāś ca vasavo'thāśvināvapi
marutaś ca sahendreṇa viśvedevās tathaiva ca
The Thirty Deities shining as fire, thumb-size, were released:
Brahmā stationed on his forehead, and Rudra was on his breast,
The Earth Protectors were on his arms, Agni was born from his mouth,
And Ādityas, Sādhyas, Vasavas, and also the Āśvins
And the Maruts with Indra and also the All-divine ones …

The kings in the *sabhā* are terrified by the vision, *nyamīlayanta netrāṇi […] trastācetasaḥ*, 'they shut their eyes, minds frightened'. I would strongly argue that this animating moment is central to our understanding of how *dhyāna* and its cosmic intimacy function, for this instant is absolutely vital in the constitution of the audience's moral awareness of the poem. For here the poem has been charged with an intellectual and spiritual tension about which the subsequent activity of *dhyāna* – as expressed between Bhīṣma and Kṛṣṇa – is established.

Kṛṣṇa revealed his being or cosmic form in a flash of theophany to the triumvirate and Saṃjaya in the *sabhā*; they were the only ones to perceive this, for Kṛṣṇa – as with Arjuna in the Gītā – had given the trio *divyaṃ cakṣur*, 'divine vision', this identical ability which Vyāsa granted to Saṃjaya (V,129,13). Thus introduced to the mystical or secret nature of the cosmos, Bhīṣma, unlike Arjuna who forgets his initiation in Book Six, is thereafter able to communicate with Kṛṣṇa in a uniquely unspeaking fashion.[10]

To expand this thesis even further and show how it concerns the way in which the epic narrative is constituted, I would argue that these two heroes are the ones to practically drive how the plot evolves and that it is their joint experience of *dhyāna* that delivers the sufficient condition here.

10 In McGrath, 2018b, I examined this mysterious relationship between Bhīṣma and Kṛṣṇa more extensively. Droṇa and Vidura, being similarly initiated by the theophany, are able – like Bhīṣma – to determine the moment of their own death, yet only Bhīṣma maintains an especial communication with Kṛṣṇa.

We have just seen how Bhīṣma, like Arjuna in the Chariot Song in Book Six, enjoys the theophanic *prakāśana*, 'radiance of illumination', or conceptual access to universal standing, yet only the elder bears throughout the poem the force of this initiation with his speech and behaviour. I am arguing that it is these two moments – *dhyānayoga* and *prakāśana* – which supply the core narrative poem with its ethical and spiritual force, what I would refer to as its 'truth'. Vyāsa oversees the former process, Kṛṣṇa Vāsudeva the latter.

In the scene in the Śānti *parvan* that we visited earlier, Bhīṣma rehearses his experience of the *sabhā* theophany, but he now describes it in the present tense: for this is what he presently perceives. He says, *paśyāmi te divyān [...] triṣu vartmasu*, 'I see your divinities among the three [cosmic] courses.' Then he adds,

> XII,51,6–7: *tac ca paśyāmi tattvena yat te rūpaṃ sanātanam [...]*
> *divaṃ te śirasā vyāptaṃ padbhyāṃ devī vasundharā*
> *diśo bhujau raviś cakṣur vīrye śakraḥ pratiṣṭhitaḥ*
> And I truly see that which is your eternal body [...]
> The sky is pervaded with your head, the divine
> earth – your feet,
> The directions – your arms, the sun – your vision,
> Śakra – stationed in [your] prowess.

This is a continuation of what was originally revealed during that first epiphanic moment during the meeting at Hāstinapura, yet this is both how and what Bhīṣma continues to apprehend concerning the immediate cosmic presence of Kṛṣṇa. Nothing like this occurs for any other hero in the poem, and certainly this kind of revelation is not part of Arjuna's life in any way.

Kṛṣṇa responds by confirming this vision of himself which the old warrior is re-experiencing, and he says,

> XII,51,10: *tato vapur mayā divyaṃ tava rājan pradarśitam*
> So – my divine body is exposed by me, O king, to you.

Now, to synthesize our two propositions: the reason that I have gone into such detail concerning the mental, spiritual and inspirational experience of these two heroes is not simply to illuminate how their telepathic communication operates but also to illustrate how it is that these two characters possess a joint or mutual volition which lies at the heart of the poem's epic narrative, one that originates from direct knowledge of the universe. They are – in terms of plot generation and conduct – the two most dynamic heroes in the poem. This, I would assert, is the immediate magnification of that originating act of *dhyāna* which Vyāsa – as a *ṛṣi* – first draws into the poem as its seminal and manifest force.

As we all know, Kṛṣṇa directs the movement of strategy and diplomacy in the poem and, as I have argued in a recent work, it is Bhīṣma who practically directs the narrative towards *bheda*, 'partition', and then continues that divisive process into the Kurukṣetra fighting. Also, it was Bhīṣma who earlier had captured Ambā, and it was this event which caused profound and vibrant repercussions that advanced the plot. Then, if Bhīṣma had not surrendered himself to the missiles of Arjuna, who was shielded by Śikhaṇḍin, the Pāṇḍavas could not have won the battle.[11] Likewise, Bhīṣma's suppression of the fact that Karṇa was the eldest born son of Kuntī and therefore the most senior of the Pāṇḍava half-brothers conduces to the destructive rivalry for the throne between taciturn Yudhiṣṭhira and the rebarbative Duryodhana.

Similarly, it was Kṛṣṇa's tactical planning during the war, concerning the killing of Ghatoṭkaca, the killing of Karṇa and the maiming of Duryodhana, that similarly assisted the Pāṇḍava triumph. Heroic Kṛṣṇa, as the *sūta* or 'charioteer' of Arjuna and in his position as virtually co-regent to *rāja* Yudhiṣṭhira, subtly dominates how the narrative or plot of the poem develops; he advises his king in discussion and he directs his hero in battle.[12] Kṛṣṇa is also the figure who oversees, if not actually performs, the second *rājasūya* rite for Yudhiṣṭhira at the outset of the Śānti *parvan* (XII,40).

To reiterate our point here, it is Kṛṣṇa and Bhīṣma who are the two most influential heroes in the epic in terms of how the plot is activated and driven and it is thus highly pertinent that they are so intellectually and emotionally united through the practice of *dhyāna*. This idea of *dhyāna* as we have seen is the activating mode of proto-inspiration for Vyāsa, and its consequence possesses vital energy for the actual evolution of the plot.[13]

There is an important exception to the above, however, for from this narrative outline I would exclude the Śānti and Anuśāsana *parvans* insofar as these two books have no narrative connection with what has preceded them

---

11 See Chapter 6.

12 In McGrath, 2017a and 2013, I discussed the nature of the dual kingship which occurs between *rāja* Yudhiṣṭhira and Kṛṣṇa. We address this point in the next chapter.

13 To draw upon a modern analogy, Bob Dylan is recorded as having described his mode of inspiration as follows: 'He clearly felt that his songs came to him from some another place and, over the years, he would come to believe that the songs were actually given to him by God. "He felt he wasn't writing songs, he was [just] writing them down," says Tom Paxton.' Sounes, 2001, p. 127, quoting Paxton from *Sing Out!* Oct.–Nov. 1962. See Thomas, 2017a and b, on the inspirational and mimetic work of Dylan the poet.

in the rest of the epic, that is, apart from the *rājasūya* rite which occurs at the outset of the former book. Bhīṣma's long discourse only begins at XII,56,1 and is virtually – in terms of narrative reference – entirely disconnected from the epic song. Within these two *parvans* there is arguably no overall narrative but only a long series of disengaged micronarratives, united simply by the fact that Bhīṣma is speaking with *rāja* Yudhiṣṭhira.

To enhance this synthesis let us now see how it is the Yādava clan who ultimately succeed after so much conflict, almost a generation of contention in fact, for both Pāṇḍava and Dhārtarāṣṭra moieties are destroyed by the fighting except for the lineage of Abhimanyu's son, Parikṣit, the grandson of Arjuna and great-nephew of Kṛṣṇa. Once the conflict and war are concluded, it is Parikṣit who holds the throne at Hāstinapura and Vajra, a lineal descendent of Kṛṣṇa, who holds that of Indraprastha; both these individuals are more genetically Yādava than anything else and so it is the Yādava matriline which has succeeded after so many years of internecine warfare. The demise of Bhīṣma terminates the Kaurava line, for he is the only direct descendent of Kuru in the central time of the poem. Our question therefore is, What concern or interest does Vyāsa have with the Yādava people?

The great Vishnu Sukthankar was the first to comment on the fact that the ancient Vedic clan of Bhṛgu must have had considerable influence upon an early classical reconfiguring of the epic. He described what he called the *Bhārgava Recension*, a hypothetical epic text which this clan somehow sponsored or patronized and in which a great number of Bhārgava myths and heroes were represented; also, this recension of the poem favoured the presence and activity of Kṛṣṇa, who moved from a position of mortal heroism to one of supernatural divinity. This classical reformation of the *Bhārata* poem, which became the *Great Bhārata*, was also profoundly disposed toward teachings of dharmic erudition, and we should not forget that the Mānava *dharmaśāstra* is delivered in the voice of ancient Bhṛgu. Ugraśravas, who is declaiming the poem in the opening lines of the *Great Bhārata*, is performing before a patron called Śaunaka, who is a direct descendent of Bhṛgu. We shall revisit this moment later, in Chapter 5.

Now, let us reiterate the important conceptual distinction between *plot* and *story*, a conceptual feature which lies at the heart of this book. The former concerns a narrative sequence where there exists a causal relation between the parts, whereas the latter concerns a narrative sequence where only a temporal relation occurs between the parts.[14]

As we have it now with the PCE text, at least 60 per cent, if not more, of the complete poem is didactic and does not portray heroic endeavour – the

14 In Aristotelian Greek these terms would be *muthos* and *praxéos*: *Poetics*, 1450a and b.

plot as it describes the action of the Pāṇḍava and Dhārtarāṣṭra protagonists. That is, this plot occupies only about 40 per cent of the whole poem as we have it today, and, carrying on from our previous point I would submit that this *plot* is in one way or another generated by Vyāsa and sustained, if not magnified, by either Kṛṣṇa or Bhīṣma, who – as we have just observed – dominate the work. It is to this plot that the Bhārgava editors introduced the materials and micronarratives which we now understand as the *story*, the part which constitutes approximately 60 per cent of the complete epic.

In the same vein, let us not forget that Paraśurāma, the arch-hero of the *Great Bhārata* and its most majestic and puissant hero, is a Bhārgava, and significantly, the only person in the poem to defeat him is Bhīṣma. Thus it is as if the Bhārgava editors have *appropriated* Bhīṣma just as they did with Kṛṣṇa in their grand design; for them, he provided the ideal *voice* for the declarations of Books Twelve and Thirteen.

Thus whatever that *ur-Bhārata* of Vyāsa had once been – what I would refer to as the early plot or the myth of the epic – developed quite early in literate times into a version of the poem which itself became modified with specific moral and political agenda into a Bhārgava apology, what I would describe as the story.[15] I would assert that the profound dhyānic unity which occurs between Bhīṣma and Kṛṣṇa was literally *essential* to this editorial agenda and was the material upon which they developed their work and which was submerged in that more classical endeavour. As we have already noted, this capacity or ability to practice *dhyāna* was something which was first introduced into that *ur*-poem by Vyāsa; he is the first one to present this activity in the poem.

As a coda to all of the above and from another point of view, there is only one scholar who has attempted to identify specifically how that early poetry of Vyāsa might have been created, and that is M. C. Smith. In her *Warrior Code of India's Sacred Song* she offered a thoroughly empirical and textually oriented model for what might have once been the proto-poem, a narrative that was firmly within the domain of late Bronze Age *kṣatriya* culture.[16]

It was her work that first led me to investigate what a possible original narrative plot might have been *like* and to consider a non-speculative methodology and thoroughly inductive medium of inference for such an inquiry, and it was Smith's work which generated the research which has led to this present study of Vyāsa. Even though the *ṛṣi* does not play a significant role in Smith's hypothetical narrative, she is the only scholar I have encountered who has

15 I have argued in McGrath, 2017a and 2018b, that such a moment occurred during the reign of Samudragupta, who flourished in the fourth century CE, 353–73.

16 M. C. Smith, 1992.

attempted to identify with a thoroughly pragmatic method and analysis how the initial Bhārata *might* have appeared; in this she formulated a narrative plot that was founded upon the use of irregular *triṣṭubh* verses. Smith extrapolated the elements of text which were expressed in this prosodic mode and – joining up the sections – generated her hypothetical proto-song, one which was predominantly *kṣatriya* in content.

The epic as it exists now thus incorporates many phases into a synchronic unity: warrior, genealogical and didactic elements having been synthesized into a single and wonderful work of art. Yet the essential plot of the poem, I would strongly aver, is a narrative close to what we think of now as the *Jaya*, the Song of Vyāsa, and what we have as a complete text nowadays is that plot *plus* all the story elements. In post-archaic and literate times, additions – supernumerous components of story – were typically placed at the end of a *parvan* or at its beginning, for reasons of scribal facility; for in a preliterate culture any introjection may be added to the poem at any time or place. This was usually how the poem was expanded, and any reader might observe this phenomenon today in the PCE.

What we now know as the *Great Bhārata* is not simply a text drawn from varying kinds of inspiration but also a text that derives from many kinds of edition, and it is this latter source of narrative – following Sukthankar – that I would credit the Bhārgava clan with, as creators and redactors of an early *Mahā*-Bhārata. Furthermore, it is at this point in time that I would assert that Vyāsa became not simply the poet of the epic but also a *character* within the poem. There is the plot, there is then the story which is made to correlate with that earlier narrative, and then there is the character himself, who through omniscience and speech acts causes the poem to advance and at other times causes the other characters to be emotionally transformed as they attend to his words. We shall examine these latter instants in Chapter 4.

In sum, for our initial thesis we examined and followed how the word *jaya* appeared in the poem and saw what it singularly referred to, and then, looking at the particular inspiration for this possible text, we analysed the poetics that were at work behind this word for Saṃjaya, who had received poetic creativity from the magic of Vyāsa. This was the first thesis.

Next, as a secondary thesis we examined the anterior condition of inspiration – the *dhyāna* of Vyāsa – which was prior to that poetic moment and then scrutinized where else this unique kind of thought occurred in the poem. This was the second thesis.

Lastly, synthesizing these two propositions, we observed how it was the presence of two especial characters in the epic practised this kind of thinking and how they determined the nature of the poem's foundational narrative or its plot. These two heroes were privileged by the Bhārgava editors in their ordering and reformation of the poem as the two figures who oversaw or controlled the basic narrative or plot, as far as we can reconstruct that today. This was our synthesis.

This is something more than the *Jaya* Song, but it is less than what we presently know as the *Great Bhārata*; for the *Jaya* is no longer a poem that can be specifically recalled or identified and thus what I have proposed and directed our attention towards in this chapter is what we now might ascertain as an outline of Vyāsa's *Bhārata.*

In sum, there is the *Bhārata*, Vyāsa's first *ideal* poem which we think of as the *Jaya* narrative; then, there exists the plot-poem of Bhīṣma and Kṛṣṇa, which rests at the intrinsic heart of the present epic; and lastly, there is the poem which includes all the genealogical and didactic components of the story.

Each of these stages or states of the poem incorporates what precedes, and these three phases are easily identifiable. The third is not the Bhārata but the *Great Bhārata*, the *Mahā*-Bhārata; whilst the first is expressly the *Jaya* Song, although this is presently beyond our recall or perception and remains purely hypothetical and yet hypostatic to the whole poem.

Thus, it would be the second model which we have depicted that comes closest to equalling what we can legitimately refer to as Vyāsa's first poem, known as the *plot* of the *Bhārata*, a narrative that now exists as the *agonistic* skeleton of the whole work.

The point of all of the above is of course not teleological, for no analyst is going to divide up the body of the epic as if it were a sacrificial victim, separating the various components of narration. The point is wholly hermeneutic, in that such research allows us to comprehend how it was that the poem has become arranged and rearranged over the millennia until what we have nowadays is a remarkable and unique work of magnificent art. It was during that long period of edition – following an earlier epoch of direct inspiration – that Vyāsa moved from being simply the first and most originally inspired poet of the work to becoming a character within the epic as it developed into a greater poem, a renewed and yet synoptic *re*-vision of that first epic song, as the initial plot became qualified by countless additional stories.

Chapter 3

TRADITIONS

HEROIC SONG traditions in late Bronze Age epic poetry demonstrate many cognate patterns, and in this light I would now like to examine two poems in particular, the Homeric Iliad and Sanskrit *Mahābhārata*.[1] The purpose of this chapter is to indicate some of the poetic milieu out of which the 'work' of the inscrutable *maximus poeta*, Vyāsa, first arose and was generated: that is, what were those poets who initially 'composed' this Vyāsa poem developing and amplifying in their song, or, what did they already *know* before they began to sing of Karṇa and Bhīṣma and heroic Kṛṣṇa?[2] What was that basic social and political template which they presumed as their poetic ground, and, what was their understanding of its poetry, those themes, concepts and perhaps even characters and social formations? How did they then allow these received models to filter into what became the Sanskrit epic as we know it today? In this sense we can consider the Sanskrit epic as a work akin to how scholars now view the Homeric Iliad, that is, as a *multitext*, a poem that is formed of many diverse yet cohering elements: historical, geographical and variously social.[3] All human culture is of course multifarious and multitudinous, and there are

---

1 A rudimentary version of this chapter was delivered in Delhi at a conference to celebrate the work of Romila Thapar. I am extremely grateful to Robert Goldman, who was the primary respondent on that occasion, for his many pertinent comments. Hiltebeitel, in 1982, pursued a similar comparative methodology, examining two geographically separated yet historically united epic traditions. Nagy, in his magnificent 2006 essay, addresses a similar formulation or perception of this tradition but in a far more encyclopaedic and compendious fashion.

2 Hellwig, 2017, p. 132, refers to the poem as 'a large anonymous text'.

3 Dué, in her remarkable 2019 research, works in this conceptual and analytic tradition. On pp. 5–6, she comments, 'The Iliad and the Odyssey are synoptic representatives of an entire system of traditional songs that developed over many hundreds of years. In its earliest phases, this system included the song traditions of the Epic Cycle and still further epic traditions to which the *Iliad* and the *Odyssey* sometimes allude, such as the voyage of the Argo, together with the mythological traditions on which those songs were based. As we will see, these song traditions were multiform. They did not exist in a fixed form until very late in their evolution. But at the same time they were traditional, in that they told the story *as it had been handed down*.'

never unique occasions – or texts – that exist apart from antecedent conditions and progressive influence; there is always continuity rather than simply a gathering of entities. The words attributed to Vyāsa adhere and comply with this model of known experience and its transmission.[4] As Gregory Nagy writes, quoting from Richard Martin, 'Good philology and intellectual honesty require the reconstruction of contexts nearest to antiquity, rather than the privileging of our own thought-worlds.'[5]

No artist, in any medium at any time, ever works without understanding and drawing upon one or more prior traditions for his or her genre.[6] To quote from Karthika Nair's inspired modern reformation of the poem, speaking of its origins the narrator says, 'Listen, this neither begins nor ends with me, not such a hate cascading down Time, crossing sea and sky and continent, a hate that sails beside friendship, love, fealty, so many skiffs. I could not say where it began, perhaps only the stars can, for beginnings come clothed in mist. There are many who will claim to know, Vyaasa foremost, but even saintly bards – especially when sons – don't allow tales to travel unadorned.'[7]

The Greek poem is more refined and is obviously now a labour of a certain degree of edition rather than of direct inspiration, whilst the latter epic is often more archaic, and in parts – as with the Kurukṣetra Books – more immediately inspired than the Homeric Iliad.[8] The *Great Bhārata* is not as purified or

4 Gerety, 2018, in his Kerala fieldwork portrays contemporary Brahminical transmission of Sāmaveda texts, demonstrating how different lineages have developed their own idiorhythmic versions of the literature. On p. 9 he writes, 'While exhibiting *idiosyncrasies in language, hermeneutics, and praxis*, these branches nevertheless partook in a widely shared textual, ritual, and religious culture that we may now broadly construe as Vedic, a culture that has persisted, in shifting forms, up to the present day.' My emphasis.

5 Nagy, personal communication, April 2019, quoting from Martin, 2018, p. 24.

6 Burgess, 2001, for instance, demonstrates how the Homeric Iliad drew upon an earlier song about the hero Memnon, assimilating narrative themes and motifs of the latter heroic poem into the song of Achilles. Apollodorus, Virgil, Shakespeare, Lönnrot, Wagner and even Bob Dylan are similar poetic artists who have informed their work with this kind of mimetic regeneration. Curiously, both Apollodorus and Virgil do not mention Odysseus and only refer to Achilles *en passant*, although both poets are deeply familiar with the forms, nature and tropes of Homeric poetry. Odysseus does appear in the summaries of the Epic Cycle, yet portrayals of him there refer to situations which are unmentioned by the two epics.

7 Nair, 2015, p. 19.

8 In the two Homeric epics, the poets commence the work and invoke the Muse who then begins the poem. These Muses are the repository of all knowledge and experience, taken from all time; they also retain an awareness of everything that can be possibly thought. This is simply what we would now call *data*, however, and does not possess the aesthetic order which is required to make information beautiful: the Muses know the *truth* but it is only through the principled direction of Apollo, the 'leader' of the Muses and source of aesthetic regulation, that a work of art is produced. In Vyāsa's case, he is

distilled in form as the Iliad, but it does offer the comparative analyst and historian far more evidence, not just about the nature of late Bronze Age culture, especially warrior or *kṣatriya* culture, but also about how those ancient poets actually worked and thought in late antiquity.[9]

The point is – unlike how some nineteenth-century Indologists once asserted that one epic tradition influenced another – that several literary customs can derive from an identical and most ancient source that is historically and culturally common to both of them. Ideally, if one wished to test this hypothesis, then the scholar would go even further back in time and study documents like the old Avestan texts to see what social models or themes were extant there.[10] As a comparative illustration of such poetic transit, describing the movement and inheritance of Homeric poetry, Bachvarova writes, 'after the fall of the Mycenaean palaces, when dialect differentiation was well under way, an inherited Greco-Aryan tradition of narrative song was lost to Attic-Ionic speakers and became confined only to Aeolic bards in Boeotia and Thessaly, who then transplanted their tradition to the coast of Anatolia in the Aeolic migrations.'[11]

In a similar vein, it is an enigma for us today why the original and generative *myth* of the *Great Bhārata* should be located at Takṣaśilā, in what is nowadays called Afghanistan, for in a logistical sense the poem situates itself mostly on the central north Indian plain of the Gangetic Doab, that is, within the environs of Kurukṣetra. What does this tell the analyst about the provenance of the early rudiments of the poem? Given the lack of strong and specific evidence of dialect trace in the present literal text, it is difficult to argue nowadays that certain parts of the epic sprang from particular regions.

If one developed the methodology of a scholar like Pargiter – who focused mainly on Purāṇic material – then an exacting study of the various clans and regional ethnicities who are present in the poem might offer indication as to an early natural distribution of parts of the work. He observed, for instance,

---

both the fount of original poetry *and* the source of its configuration; this is an important distinction concerning poetic inspiration as it relates to the two traditions of epic song. Apart from what we have discussed concerning *dhyāna*, in the Indic system there is no characterization of primary inspiration except perhaps for the *ākāśa*, 'subtle space', but this is without representation. As we have observed earlier, for poets like Saṃjaya the act of 'seeing' precedes anything that is acoustically inspirational: sight conduces to hearing, in terms of diachrony.

9 West, 2007, pp. 63–68 and 470–95, views the Indo-European parallels that exist in the Homeric Iliad, Epic *Mahābhārata* and Rāmāyaṇa.

10 Skjærvø, 2000; West, 2007; Frame, 2009; Watkins, 1995; and Bachvarova, 2016; to name a few, have worked in this field of archaic comparative research.

11 Bachvarova, 2016, pp. 402–3.

that '[m]uch of the strength of the Kauravas lay in the assistance which they received from the north-western countries'.[12] Likewise, he noted, "The nations in and around the Panjab formed a very strong portion of the Kaurava confederacy.'[13] In this light, in my book on *rāja* Yudhiṣṭhira I tracked the evidence surrounding the kingdom of Magadha, but the reference was so irregular and random that such pursuit was inconclusive.[14]

Any reader of the poem will immediately realize that the *style*, not only of narration but also of the Sanskrit language itself, varies greatly from *parvan* to *parvan* and sometimes even from *upākhyāna* to *upākhyāna*, the 96 'micronarratives'. Whatever the regional sources of the dramatic elements, narrative components, the ingredients of story and perhaps even of certain characters in the poem, this area of research remains untouched: the geography and ethnicities of the *Great Bhārata* continue to remain an unknown dimension of the work. For instance, characters like Karṇa or Duryodhana might have become degraded in time whilst others, like Arjuna or Paraśurāma, have advanced in literary and heroic status.

Perhaps the heroes were once topographically or provincially generated. Just as the plot origins of the Homeric Iliad appear to have moved from the Anatolian East towards the Mediterranean coast and thence towards mainland Attica as they accrued variation, so too the *Bhārata* became a likely constellation of diverse locative backgrounds.[15] Gāndhārī, the mother of the Dhārtarāṣṭras, is certainly of that older Āryan terrain of Afghanistan, whereas Karṇa becomes *rāja* of Aṅga in the East. Cedi, Kamboja, Kaśi, Kuru, Kaliṅga, Matsya and Yādava, to name a few of the important allied armies present at Kurukṣetra, need much closer historical analysis if we – as close readers – are going to comprehend how the affiliations and contentions of the poem occur both practically and materially. How are we to perceive the causality at work in how heroes were born in such regions, and also, *with whom* do those specific heroes typically find themselves engaged? Yet it is the obfuscation of these topical elements which led to the poem becoming pan-Indic and a *classical* text for the subcontinent.[16]

---

12 Pargiter, 1908, p. 318. He continues, on p. 20, to say that 'only one leading king from Madhyadeśa supported the Kauravas, namely Bhūriśravas, but it is difficult to make out his position'. On pp. 332–33, Pargiter lists the various 'nations' and how they allied with either the Pāṇḍavas or the Dhārtarāṣṭras.

13 Pargiter, 1908, p. 336.

14 Even Sörensen in his *Index of Names* affirmed the confusion that enveloped any mention of these people in the poem.

15 'The Pāṇḍavas' centre was Upaplavya, the capital of Matsya, and the Kaurava centre was their own capital at Hastināpura.' Pargiter, 1908, p. 335.

16 A scholar like Keith, 1908, p. 835, would even assert, 'Some of the tradition may reflect vaguely the ancient contest of the Tṛtsu-Bharatas against the other Aryan tribes,

I have argued in the past that it was just not possible for a single author or even a 'committee' to have accomplished a seamless amalgamation of such a centripetal gathering of poetry, however stylized is the action of Vyāsa.[17] It was the preliterate tradition itself which, over more than a millennium, accomplished this *streamlined* achievement, and it was due to centuries of poets performing in agonistic situations – probably at ritual festivals – that the many works of inspiration slowly became refined and then compounded into a unified work of literate edition, one that might have been planned and arranged in one single location, perhaps at Pāṭaliputra.

The two robust works of art here in question derive from an ancient tradition of Āryan poetry, and both of these heroic texts – the Iliad and the *Great Bhārata* – are now what we would refer to as a *classic*, that is, they have become repositories or stores of cultural worth and record.[18] During this process of becoming Panhellenic or Pan-Indic there was a reduction in social specificity, and conversely, there was incorporated into the poetry a great range of geographical material which conduced to the poems becoming a common possession of not simply one locale or regime. Even historical particularity was elided from the poetry in this endeavour to become geopolitically uniform. In the present *Great Bhārata* we now observe Vedic divinities in the company of supernal figures drawn from nascent Hinduism as well as a wide spectrum of simultaneously various political institutions; that is, the poem is a composite, a synthesis of many disparate and a-historical parts. It was within this milieu that Vyāsa – or the poets who originally shaped Vyāsa – worked both as a creator and as a character.

Obversely, due to this *classical* impulse much that was truly historical has been occluded from these epics and this, I would argue, is a consequence of

---

equally bearers of the Vedic traditions, and in this sense we may believe in a Kuru epic before the Pāṇḍavas appear [...] The most probable theory seems to me that the Pāṇḍavas were a northern, perhaps semi-Mongolian tribe who succeeded in winning the leading position among the Bharatas.'

17 In a search for what he refers to as textual *stratification*, Hellwig, 2017, has analysed the poem using digital algorithmic means that process the grammatical arrangement of the epic. On p. 144, he demonstrates how the four Kurukṣetra Books, along with the Sauptika *parvan*, employ the imperfect form with more frequency than any other *parvan*, with the exception of the Mausala.

18 Deshpande, 1978, p. 1–2, writes, 'The *Mahābhārata* has not only influenced the literature, art, sculpture and painting of India but it has also moulded the very character of the Indian people. Characters from the Great Epic [...] are still household words [...] and these characters stand for domestic or public virtues or vices [...] In India a philosophical or even political controversy can hardly be found that has no reference to the thought of the *Mahābhārata* [...] It would not be an exaggeration to say that the people of India have learnt to think and act in terms of the *Mahābhārata*.'

edition rather than of poetic inspiration; it is for this reason that Pargiter's method of exploration or analysis is one that faces serious constraints. That early first-millennium society which the poems represent has been, in the case of India, stripped of all indication of Buddhism, for instance, even though during that period Buddhism as a culture was flourishing throughout much of South Asia.[19] The same is true of the geopolitical reality of the Eastern Mediterranean during a mid-first-millennium period where particular historical conditions – as with the predominance of Athens, for instance – have been strangely elided from the poetry.

Similarly, I find it difficult to accept that during the first millennium there was no social memory, recollection or any mention of artefacts from the vast Indus Valley Civilization; there is absolutely no indication of such in our present Pune Critical Edition (PCE) of the epic or in any of the other various textual traditions. For me, there is something 'unnatural' in that omission and it signifies a particular exclusive ambition of those early editors. This too I would explain as being due to the forces of *classical impulse*, the decision to produce a work that was thoroughly inclusive – and perhaps hegemonic – and yet with a distinctly exclusive political agenda. I have argued elsewhere that such a historical moment occurred during the period of Gupta hegemony, particularly during the reign of Samudragupta.[20]

To explain the identities between two or more literary traditions, one can either assert a conjoint migratory ancestry in which a common primaeval source of social or poetic modelling continues into later works of poetic art; here it is not the case that one system of poetry can influence another but that they both possess a mutually similar social origin. Or, one can ascribe this community of modelling to morphological acculturation, whereby one tradition is incorporated by another tradition not by physically human migration but simply by a transit of ideas. Let me now present nine general points that demonstrate explicit communities and disparities between these two late Bronze Age epic songs; these are elements – both social and poetic – which the 'Vyāsa poets' knew and naturally involved in what became the *Bhārata* poem.

Firstly, let us quickly review certain qualities of life in these two poems. In both of the societies portrayed by these great works the cultures are preliterate

---

19 See Verardi, 2011.

20 McGrath, 2017a, p. 28–29. Deshpande, 1978, p. 10, offers a more contemporary and particular expression of such *classicism*, one which can be observed during the early printing of the texts: 'The *Mahābhārata* was printed for the first time in 1834–39 at Calcutta by the Asiatic Society of Bengal and subsequently in 1863 and 1913 by Ganapat Krishnaji and Gopal Narayan respectively at Bombay [...] These editions were not based on any critical principles. Manuscripts that could be available to the editors were used indiscriminately.'

and premonetary, that is, there was no writing nor was there any money, and culture then was most certainly thoroughly non-secular. As we know, the first condition had great import for the nature of how these poems were composed, performed and transmitted, whilst the second condition underlies all political and economic formations as displayed within these epic songs. Let us recall that preliteracy and premonetary culture disappeared with the advent of secondary urbanization in India.

Similarly, there is no significant architecture in these two poems nor is there any formal or solemn ritual, and there is certainly no *pūjā* in the *Great Bhārata.* Kṛṣṇa does mention such a kind of worship in his Chariot Song in Book Six, but *pūjā* does not exist as a practice in the narrative; there is no sculpture either, an essential component for such devotional rites.[21] In the Homeric Iliad, sacrificial occasions take place outside, beneath the sky and what few priests appear are more *mantic* or prophetic rather than masters of orthoprax ceremony; there are no temples.

Let us also recall that many of the figures in this epic poetry are inhuman, that is, they are not born solely of mortal parents. The Pāṇḍava half-siblings; Droṇa; Draupadī and her brother; Achilles and Sarpedon – to name a few characters – are semi-divine or actually completely non-human; yet they *appear* and *act* as if they were men and women. Characters like Vyāsa himself, Nārada or Rāma Jāmadagnya are likewise more-than-mortal, and their lives are in fact undying.

Thus the world of these epics is artificial and certainly non-historical despite the fact that it *seems* to be familiar and akin to our world, the world of the audience. Deities walk with the heroes and heroines and they speak together, dine together and sometimes make love or fight with each other in this composite depiction of an idealized period in ancient time. Yet these simulated late Bronze Age societies are wholly created by the poets and later modified by the poems' editors; they do not reflect any material reality except perhaps in weaponry or charioteering, for there is little actual material culture evident in these works.[22] It is, as we mentioned earlier, this complete degree of artifice which conduces towards that poetic status of a *classic*, for there is nothing strongly restricted to any region or historical social group in these two epics. Even the characters in Vyāsa's poem and the Homeric Iliad display little evidence of physical appearance, as with physiognomy, for instance, and there is no weather in this poetry.

---

21 See McGrath, 2016, ch. 3, n. 46, for a list of all passing mentions of likely statuary in the Sanskrit poem.

22 Unlike the *Great Bhārata*, there is little chariot fighting in the Homeric Iliad, except for some scant mentions in Scroll V.

What we as readers now see is a unique and syncretic culture that is played upon the margin which exists between life and death, for that is the region where the mortal heroes die and where the eternal deities appear and disappear.[23] In terms of place this is inherently construed as either Kurukṣetra or Troy.[24] I would assert, therefore, that the *Bhāratavarṣa* of the Sanskrit poem is, on the one hand, purely a fiction of poetry and metaphor and, on the other, a portrait of a world or universe that exceeds all material conceptions of quotidian reality due to the artistic *finesse* of the Vyāsa poet or poets whose vision created this deathless song of human and cosmic truth. Both Troy and Kurukṣetra are works that originate in the minds of many generations of poets and are not to be retrieved in a physical sense.

Secondly, concerning time, even the certainty of time and linear duration in these epics is, to paraphrase Romila Thapar, 'metaphorical', for there are many *kinds* or forms of time; it is never a constant. Time in both the *Great Bhārata* and Homeric Iliad is simultaneously multifold, polytropic and never uniform, which for us as modern readers appears unreasonable, for time in these two poems is a matrix for many differing planes of narrative that occur simultaneously. Let us examine just a few of these dimensions.[25]

In the *Mahābhārata* there is the universal time of the *yugas* which embraces all other temporal cycles and sequences. Also, in both the Greek and Sanskrit epics there is the time which the deities and ancestors inhabit, which is beyond the worldly envelope of the mortal heroes, an envelope into which the divinities occasionally enter. Then there is the performative nature of time itself; as we have already noted, in the *Great Bhārata*, Ugraśravas opens the song and speaks of how his words engage with what Vyāsa once said and which Vaiśaṃpāyana then recorded and within which Saṃjaya tells of his perceptions. This series of voices in itself embraces many various facets of temporal registry, for Saṃjaya lived four generations before Vaiśaṃpāyana, and the latter is two generations before Ugraśravas who then performs his work.

---

23 Thomas Hardy in his preface to *The Dynasts* (1910) referred to the act of reading as 'mental performance'.

24 There are five central localities involved in the *Great Bhārata* narrative: Hāstinapura, Indraprastha, the forest, Matsya country and Kurukṣetra. It is the latter which is the place that dominates the mood of the poem, however, as a place of death. It was there that Paraśurāma destroyed the *kṣatriyas*, that Bhīṣma defeated Paraśurāma, that the terrible internecine battle occurred, and it was there that the supine Bhīṣma delivered his great oration.

25 On this point I would urge the interested reader to consult my 'Appendix on Epic Time', in McGrath, 2017a, pp. 189–206, and also the final chapter in McGrath, 2018b, 'Note on Poetics'. In Chapter 7 below, the nature of time in the Homeric Odyssey is specifically described.

There are also seven generations inclusively between Śaṃtanu and Janamejaya, a temporal hierarchy that the poem literally reverses insofar as the epic concludes with the ritual that is said to have inspired the first singing of the *Bhārata*, thus creating the illusion of a cycle. This is what we can refer to as 'poetic time', an aesthetic and moral constitution of the temporal.

Fundamentally, time is constituted by transition, by serial connectivity supplied by metonym, and where there occurs a shift in the narrative – something that happens frequently in the *Great Bhārata* – there exists a disjunctive moment in narrative metonymy which is contrary to the usual temporal advance: suddenly another story is being performed and the metonyms shift to another register of signification. Hence the sequence of events in the poetry is often random and does not denote any movement of serial time at all, and there are dislocations between events in the narrative, as in the Ādi *parvan*, for instance. This leaves the audience with a distinct sense of *bricolage*, and it is as if the story had been oddly composed without any regard to linear development where temporal unities are to be respected. To quote again from Thapar, the *Mahābhārata* 'is no longer only the story of the feud and war, but has acquired a number of episodes (some of which are unrelated to the main story)'.[26]

As we observed earlier, in certain areas of the narrative, as in the Kurukṣetra Books, there is terrific use of metaphor and simile to such an extent that almost 80 per cent of the poetry has little narrative consequence. The world of simile is of course timeless and unchanging, almost in an *ekphrastic* sense, for it is a fixed and unworldly conception. In the Śānti *parvan* there is virtually no serial time at all as transitions of day and night are not registered and the materials of that book and the subsequent Anuśāsana *parvan* have no actual chronological relation with what preceded them in the epic's previous eleven books. These parts of the epic are thus presented as literally or actually 'timeless'.

The above points are just some of the timely dimensions of the work which is associated with Vyāsa and his subsequent poets or, obversely, some of the aspects associated with the poets who created and generated the idea of Vyāsa as poet and character. It is as if time in the *Mahābhārata* is often more a figure of structural form rather than of temporal development. Whereas in the Homeric Iliad there is a bare sequence of days – forty days, in fact – the subject of that period bears little significance in terms of plot, as most of the poem is only story, so that serial time becomes etiolated.

Thirdly, I would like to address a most significant point first raised by Thapar, who long ago commented on how the Yādava clan were disposed towards a system of matrilineal kinship; this is a point that we touched upon

26 Thapar, 2002, p. 102.

in the previous chapter.[27] Indo-Āryan society was typically patrilineal in its kinship alignment, and this is generally the kind of lineage scheme that is apparent in the Homeric Iliad. What exists in the *Great Bhārata*, however, is different and twofold.

Matrilineal systems of kinship are typically endogamous, whereas the patrilineal are usually exogamous; or, to quote from Thomas Trautmann's famous essay, 'In a word, the Dravidian kinship system obliges one to marry a relative, the Indo-Aryan obliges one to marry a "stranger".'[28] It is highly pertinent, therefore, as well as socially determinative that in an earlier Bhārata time when Paraśurāma exterminated the *kṣatriyas* on 21 separate occasions, it was the remaining widowed *kṣatriya* women who in this extreme situation regenerated their *varṇa*, 'caste', by becoming impregnated by *brāhmaṇa* men (I,58,5–7). Thus the warrior lineage only descended *via* the feminine side. This is an important social template for the poem and is what I would aver was a central theme in Vyāsa's primary composition. As we have remarked above, the failed and terminal Dhārtarāṣṭra lineage descends from Vyāsa, whereas the lineage of Janamejaya can be construed as descending from the earlier position of Satyavatī's brother.

The Pāṇḍava half-brothers and the Dhārtarāṣṭra sons manifest two paradigms of kinship formation. The former, being descended from Kuntī, are in the matrilineal style, whilst the latter, being descended from old blind Dhṛtarāṣṭra, express a social manifold that is patrilineal. The clan which succeeds after the terrible war and mutual annihilation at Kurukṣetra are Yādava scions, descendants of Kuntī: Parikṣit is established in Hāstinapura and Vajra at Indraprastha.[29] Genetically, both these young warriors are more Yādava than anything else; such is their physiological inheritance.

Let us likewise recall that of all the heroes in the poem only Bhīṣma is a lineal descendent of Kuru and the term 'Kaurava' is simply a nominal indicator of the inhabitants of a geographical area; it was merely a metonym that has become a toponym and bears no lineal sense of filial disposition.

The conflict in the first part of the *Great Bhārata* is thus one that occurs between two kinds of lineage paradigm: the matriline versus the patriline, with the former moiety triumphing. The situation of *bheda* or 'partition' which was

27 Thapar, 1978, pp. 260–1: 'The Yādava kinship system shows traces of matrilineal structure which is alien to the Indo-European kinship system.'

28 Trautmann, 1974, pp. 61–62: 'A rule of cross-cousin marriage (i.e. marriage with one's mother's brother's daughter, one's father's sister's daughter, or their terminological equivalents) is typical of Dravidian-speaking groups; it is incompatible with the Indo-Aryan rules of exogamy as propounded in the brahminical law-books.'

29 Vajra is a lineal descendent of Kṛṣṇa, most likely a grandson.

first proposed by ancient Bhīṣma in the *sabhā* is only resolved at that point of victory when the division is terminated.[30] Also, at that point of resolution, the division in the clan which began with the separation of the sons of primordial Yayāti – Yadu and Pūru – is likewise reconciled.

It is curious that the side of the victorious clan, which practises matrilineal affinity, is the Pāṇḍava moiety whilst the strictly patrilineal Dhārtarāṣṭras are the ones to lose all in the conflict. The Pāṇḍavas are of course extremely family oriented and the audience hears much about their domestic and sometimes intimate relations, whereas for the Dhārtarāṣṭras there is virtually no mention of marital or household life and – almost without exception – they are all male. Vyāsa, as we shall see, moves his original allegiance from the Dhārtarāṣṭras towards the Pāṇḍavas.

In the Homeric Iliad I have not been able to discern such a profound tension between kinship groups, one that fuels the narrative force with its drive; for there the patrilineal is the model of kinship for both of the opposing sides who are fighting on the fields at Troy: Priam, Agamemnon, Hector and Achilles all demonstrate a non-matrilineal form of affinity. Our next point will explain why this is the case. However, it is only on the Trojan side that women participate in the social discourse of the warriors, with Hecuba, Andromache and Helen all contributing to verbal exchanges. Among the Achaeans the only woman to speak – and that is confined to one single lament – is Briseis. Thetis, Athena, Aphrodite, Hera and Iris do speak directly, but they are not mortal.

Fourthly, how is it that a record of warrior experience, a song, becomes imperishable and undying? Is it the medium itself which achieves this or is it the unique individuality of how these heroes and heroines lived and died? Likewise, does heroic perception of this border between the eternal and the diurnal, between the world beyond death and the world of the living, inform us in any way about the nature of the universe? What actually is the truth which is borne by the *Great Bhārata*, a work of fiction, or how is it that moral truth can be conveyed by the fiction of poetry, a fiction that bears no relation with any historical event?

Examining this point concerning epic poetics from another aspect, what initially drew me to a study of the *Great Bhārata* was the character of Karṇa, a hero who – like Achilles in the Homeric Iliad – is prepossessed by the potence and clarity of his *kīrti*, 'fame'. In Greek this word is *kléos*, and both words etymologically indicate a phenomenon that is to be *heard*.[31] That is, both of

---

30 Bhīṣma is the first to propose the idea of *bheda* at I,195,8.

31 See Watkins, 1995, chs 8 and 15 – especially the latter, concerning Vedic *śrávas ákṣitam*, 'imperishable fame'.

these heroes are deeply concerned with the nature of their enduring report and how it will survive and magnify their worldly experience as warriors on earth. It is the durability of the 'song' which presents their deeds as warriors, and it is this which preoccupies them far more than their longevity as living beings.

This is, in a sense, a passion that is actually transcendental, for both heroes are only interested in that which is eternal, their *kīrti* or *kléos*, and neither are especially concerned with the *réalia* of mortal and earthly life. As we shall soon observe, Vyāsa, as the originator and first proponent of this *kīrti*, then proceeds to direct the drama of the poem as the narrative expands and develops.

Thus both the heroes, Karṇa and Achilles, are profoundly engaged with the intrinsic magnetism of epic poetry, or the medium of their 'fame', and for us today, studying the narratives of these two warriors illustrates how the poetry of *kṣatriya* epic – as generated and then supervised by Vyāsa – functions either in performance or in its status as a repository of heroic experience and classically formulated value. That experience is one that uniquely dramatizes what it means to live and to die; for if one can stylize and precisely depict death as an instant, what one is simultaneously portraying – obversely – is the origin of consciousness itself.

This frontier between death and human consciousness concerns the drama which both Achilles and Karṇa endure, not simply as warriors but as mortal and transient human beings whose time on earth is closely delimited. They live only in exchange for the *song*, that is, in exchange for this idea of imperishable *fame* or epic narrative. It is this particular and personal economy of metaphor which completely preoccupies them as heroes rather than any achievement which might be humanly sensible or proficient under the sun. Fame for a hero is not a martial consideration but something which concerns their verbal presence within an endurable narrative.

Fifthly, addressing kingly polities as manifest in the *Mahābhārata* and Iliad, there is the phenomenon of *dyarchy* or dual kingship which obtains in both of these epic songs. What we observe in the *Great Bhārata* is a vehicle of double kingship between Yudhiṣṭhira and Kṛṣṇa, where the former assumes the ritual roles of governance whilst the latter is more a martial and diplomatic figure. *Rāja* Yudhiṣṭhira is very much a *sacrificer* in the *Mahābhārata* with his three central rites: the *rājasūya*, the *śastrayajña* and the *aśvamedha*.[32] Strangely, the first ceremony occurs twice, before the battle and then after the conclusion of so

32 In McGrath, 2015a, I portray a modern *rāja* who holds a similar position of ritualist.

much dreadful war, once at Indraprastha and once at Hāstinapura, and it is as if there were almost what we might consider as a *double kingdom.*[33]

Kṛṣṇa serves as both *dūta*, 'herald' or 'ambassador', as well as being one who guides and oversees the conduct of warfare. He is never *senāpati*, 'commander of the armies', but his subtle oversight concerning strategy and tactics is what wins the battle at Kurukṣetra for the Pāṇḍavas and simultaneously destroys the Dhārtarāṣṭras.

In the Homeric Iliad this ancient model of the double kingship exists between two brothers, Agamemnon and Menelaos.[34] Although the former is the paramount commander of the Greek army, it is Menelaos who actually participates more in combat duelling, whilst Agamemnon is the only hero to carry a *máxaira*, 'dagger', and it is with this that he performs sacrifices.[35] Sparta, in classical times, was famed for its double kingship, and in early Rome a similar political model was also practiced.[36] It is telling that the institution is present in the first half of the *Great Bhārata*. I would argue, however, that this kind of establishment came to an end once the use of money was developed and became widespread.[37]

In the Homeric Iliad, supreme political authority is signalled by two terms for chief or king, *wánax* and *basiléus*.[38] I would propose that the latter word indicates a hereditary style whereas the former title concerns a chief among other leaders. This is only so during a period of preliteracy, however, for once writing and money are fabricated society and political economy change rapidly

---

33 In McGrath, 2016, I showed how *doubleness* or *duality* is a constant theme in the *Great Bhārata* and was a mnemonic means by which the poets worked as they produced their work.

34 Il.I, 16.

35 Agamemnon bears a *máxaira* solely for the purposes of ritual killing (III, 271). I would urge the reader to consult the popular site, http://greekmythcomix.com/comic/deaths-in-the-iliad-a-classics-infographic/, for a near-comprehensive summary of personal *kills* in the Homeric Iliad. It would be a telling statistic if similar figures were available for the four Kurukṣetra Books of the *Bhārata* poem.

36 I have described this phenomenon of *dyarchy* in McGrath, 2013; and 2017a, ch. I,iii. Dumézil, 1940 and 1977, has portrayed this dual tradition as it occurs in other political cultures, notably the Roman. Thucydides in his *History*, in Scroll I, writes of the practice of double kingship as it obtained in classical Sparta.

37 In the ten 'History Plays' of Shakespeare, where the long contest for a crown is dramatically enacted, there is always a good or 'natural' king and the *bad* or tyrannical king; usually it is the latter who dies so that the former might flourish, the former being the Tudor monarchs.

38 In the *Great Bhārata* the term *rāja* is non-specific or unmarked and can be translated as 'lord'; it is almost an honorific title. The specific appellation denoting paramount kingship is *nṛpatir*; see McGrath, 2017a, ch. I,vii.

and profoundly and the old systems of fidelity and loyalty are supplanted by a scheme founded not on an exchange of services but on an exchange of money. Then, kingship assumes another title, that of the *túrannos*, which is how kings were designated in the later and classical Athenian dramas.

In India there was no such lexical translation indicating that shift towards individual monarchy. What we can observe, however, are two *designs* of kingship, as evinced, on the one hand, by the first eleven books of the *Great Bhārata* and, on the other, by the *type* of royal polity as represented in the recumbent Bhīṣma's two books, the Śānti and Anuśāsana *parvans*, where the establishment of kingship has moved away from a dependence on personal loyalty and fealty to one of employment where a king's followers were to be paid.[39] I would submit that the second half of the *Mahābhārata* is a text that was established during a period of literacy whilst the first eleven books portray a kind of social, economic and political life that was preliterate.[40] The presence and activity of Vyāsa during the latter period and its particular composition is much *weaker*, as we have seen.

This constitutional model is further complicated in the Indian epic, for among one moiety of the clan, that of the Pāṇḍava half-brothers, the family of *rāja* Yudhiṣṭhira establishes what is in effect a fraternal direction of rule, one that works in close company with the leading members of the community; I have described this in detail in a recent book.[41]

This is a kind of archaic polity which historians have referred to as the *saṅgha*, an 'association', where the *kula* or 'clan' is the significant social unit and where the king is more of an oligarchic chief rather than a unique sovereign figure, which is how we usually consider the ideal of kingship today. These political groups are similar to what Bhīṣma refers to – during the first part of his long oration – as *gaṇas*, when he accounts for *rājyadharma*. For an historian like Agrawala, the terms *saṅgha* and *gaṇa* were synonyms.[42]

Nothing like this is apparent in the Homeric Iliad, where it is obvious that Agamemnon is personally decisive in his kingship; for example, in Scroll

39 See Thapar, 1992, p. 149: 'the Sabhāparvan, encapsulating the essence of a lineage society, stands in contrast to the Śāntiparvan with its rhetoric on the monarchic state.'

40 Hellwig, in his wonderful 2017 article, on p. 164 expresses this phenomenon as an example of what he calls 'stratification', when he observes, 'how closely low-level linguistic features of a text are correlated with topic structure,' and that these can represent 'diachronic trends in linguistics'.

41 McGrath, 2017a, ch. I,ii and II,ii. The fraternal system of kingship as revealed by the epic is *like* the modern system of kingship that exists in Saudi Arabia today, where the kings are all sons of Ibn Saud. That is, until the next succession, when another generation will take account.

42 Agrawala, 1952, p. 428.

I when the army wishes to surrender Chryseis to her father, who has come to ransom her return, once Agamemnon interdicts this desire no one contests his command, not even Menelaos. There is a consensus here concerning the king's authority even though the community disagrees with him, whereas in the *Great Bhārata* there are endless discussions among the half-brothers and Draupadī concerning what *should* be done in terms of policy; there is always much *argument*, to paraphrase Amartya Sen, before any decision is reached. Then, however, it is usually Kṛṣṇa who actually implements the policy.

Sixthly, in both of these ancient epic poems the narrative – both practically and verbally – is generated by the movement of women. In the case of the Iliad it is the physical movement of Helen, of Chryseis and of Briseis which effects the narrative as we know it today. For Epic *Mahābhārata* it is the movement of Draupadī into the *sabhā* and her abject treatment in that situation which causes the poem to procede: this is the source of the epic's plot. Likewise, in both the Rāmāyana and Homeric Odyssey it is the position of a woman which also drives the narrative movement forward in time.

Let us not forget, however, that it was another woman whose action supplied the primary necessary condition for all the ensuing conflict in *bhāratavarṣa*: for it was Kuntī's suppression of the fact that the eldest of her sons was Karṇa, who therefore should – by the right of seniority – have been king, that supplied the sufficient condition for all the contention between moieties.

Also, Śakuntalā, Sāvitrī, Draupadī and queen Kuntī, to name a few of the Bhārata women, all possess voices that remind and propel their menfolk according to what is correct *kṣatriya dharma*; they are the ones to know what is 'right action' and what should be accomplished in times of uncertainty and irresolution. They are what I have referred to elsewhere as speakers of truth.[43]

On a further note of likeness, the heroines Draupadī, Sītā and Penelope all conduct *svayaṃvaras* as a means to select a potential groom.[44] It is as if certain key feminine figures in these epics bear an especial cultural valence or worth in the manner in which their actions generate and enact the procession of the plot.

As there is no *money* in these epic societies but only quantities of movable wealth, I have argued elsewhere that it is the presence of these valuable women which acts as a standard of value, much like the gold standard used to operate a century ago in world trade.[45] In narrative terms, these women stand for the ultimate index of human valence in warrior culture and they act as a

---

43 McGrath, 2011, ch. V.

44 Jamison, 1994, has written extensively on this theme.

45 McGrath, 2011.

token that impels the poetry onward through time; in fact, they are the source of the poem's development.

Thus the conflict in both of these epics centres upon the value of women, and it is notable that material wealth is mentioned in Epic *Mahābhārata* particularly on the occasion of marital union.[46] It is as if the presence and bearing of the feminine in these poems act as signs of material exchange, for in a premonetary economy no single registration of value exists. In the Homeric Iliad, movable wealth is mentioned when certain women are being ransomed and they are always connected with the idea of a *price.*[47]

Seventhly, advancing our second and earlier point about time as a metaphor, let us recall that Epic *Mahābhārata* is not a narrative about *dharma*, but to the contrary, it practically concerns a world of *adharma*. In the cosmogonic cycle the Kali *yuga*, only one quarter of all possible goodness or just equilibrium is possible, for – as both the epic and the Mānava *dharmaśāstra* tell us – worldly order is only possible in a quartile form at that point in universal time.[48] It is heroic Kṛṣṇa, the charioteer, who, mounted on his vehicle, informs Karṇa about the incipience of the new and most dreadful *yuga* (V,120,34). During such a historic or temporal period *all* human action, in terms of behaviour, speech and thought, can only be *dharmic* in one fourth: that is all.

Thus what we as an audience observe is not so much a conflict of *dharma* in the first eleven books of the poem but a contention between *adharma* and *adharma*: *dharma* here being a matter of semantics whereas *adharma* is a consideration of judgement.[49] What is expressed by Bhīṣma during his long two-month oration concerns what *should* occur, that is, he is expressing hundreds of *dharmic* models: social, political, economic, spiritual, ritual and esoteric. In terms of what is *just* then, the first half of the Sanskrit epic and its second half address completely different juridical systems and apprehensions of justice.

To draw upon the thought of Amartya Sen here, the Pāṇḍavas formulate their conception of what is *right* according to how it is that they perceive *injustice*: it is their perception of *wrong* which supplies them with their particular understanding of what should be rightful *dharma*.[50]

---

46 McGrath, 2011, ch. II.

47 In the Homeric Odyssey the drama of the second half of the poem moves about the figure of Penelope and the question as to whom she is going to marry. Again, we observe this focal position of the feminine in terms of how the narrative is organized about the centripetal figure of a high-status woman for whom all the men compete. See the final chapter to this present book.

48 Mānava *Dharmaśāstra* II,3; and *Mahābhārata* X,2,1.

49 In McGrath, 2018b, ch. 4, I have written at length concerning this question of *adharma* and *dharma* in Epic *Mahābhārata*.

50 Sen, 2009, p. vii.

One can perceive such a contest of *adharma* in the Homeric Iliad, where there are contentious views as to what 'should' be the *price* of a woman and, likewise, what should be the retribution that is offered for an improper appropriation of a woman – for there is no single standard of correct or *right* behaviour there. On the Shield of Achilles in Scroll XVIII, this terrible complexity or irresolution is visually exhibited, where there occurs a small scene in which two men contest over the 'blood-price', *poinē*, for a dead kinsman. This price is of course not to be represented by money but by movable wealth.[51]

To take this point further or to view this idea of legal contention from another aspect, what occurs in our two poems, Homeric Iliad and Epic *Mahābhārata*, concerns a juridical system of mutual retribution or 'mirror vengeance', what in Latin was once termed as *lex talionis* or 'reciprocal violence'. This is completely *unlike* the Hebrew or Mosaic structure of jurisprudence where right is categorically stated in an exactly certain fashion, for there it was what we refer to as *codified.* So the Pāṇḍava half-brothers seek revenge for what they view as an injustice, yet what exists in the vast and diverse monologue of the Śānti and Anuśāsana *parvans* is a legal order that is founded upon a king's judgement and not upon a template of vendetta: these are two separate forms of jurisdiction.[52]

To briefly revert to the plot of the Homeric Iliad, it is this economy of metaphors – the conceived value of *right* in terms of an exchange which compensates for a perceived wrong – which drives the poem. These exchanges ultimately concern the one quality or token of value which mentally and emotionally charges a warrior like Achilles with the question, 'What is the value of a human life?' For most of the epic narrative this concerns the movement of three particular women, but for the superb Achilles the question is the moral valence of his own life cycle. He will of course complete the economy of metaphors by exchanging his life for *kléos*, or *kīrti*, 'fame', which as we know – from our fourth point above – refers to the medium of epic song itself; for heroes this is the only signifier of worth or value in the cosmos.[53]

Eighthly, I would like to focus not so much on the poetry of these two wonderful works of art but on their ritual consequences, particularly as this concerns their performance. This is to examine not the sources of Vyāsa's

51 Prisoners are not a social category in the *Great Bhārata*, whereas they figure significantly in the military economy of Homeric Iliad on the occasions when *ápoina*, 'ransom', is paid for their return.

52 See McGrath, 2018b, p. 94. In the Hesiodic Works and Days, there is a curious absence of jurisdiction by vendetta and only the judgement of kings receives description.

53 This economy of metaphors is constituted by a series of exchanges: anger > violence > death > grief lamentation > epic song.

inspiration but the direction of his work, its social projection or the *ethics* of the practice of poetry.

For instance, it is commonplace in the Kurukṣetra Books for Saṃjaya to engage with metaphors and similes that reflect sacrificial procedure, where heroes are often likened to the *ghee* that is poured as an oblation upon a ritual fire. The terrific battle ardour, the 'martial rage' or *krodha* of the heroes in combat is such that the flaring of the oblation is akin to the wrath of the militant heroes as they are perceived in terrific warfare.

Similarly, in the Greek epic the poets often say that during such occasions of heroic violence the warrior actually becomes *daímoni īsos*, 'like a deity', such is the intense brilliance and vitality of their martial dynamism.[54] That is, the warrior during this instance of ultimate rage – just like the ritual oblation – moves closer towards an immortal condition, for in that brief moment of death there is an occasion of unearthly or inhuman translation towards a condition which is *more-than-mortal*: at their moment of death heroes become akin to the supernatural.[55] What this means in pragmatic terms is that they live on in song and poetry, the medium of their immortality, constantly re-enacting this proximity with the divine, which is then sometimes replayed in practical ritual when devotees offer worship at the shrines dedicated to their cults.

For instance, in the Homeric Iliad there is a vital scene in Scroll XVI when Patroclus, the charioteer of Achilles, is felled. He dies in a threefold manner, receiving three separate strikes: from Apollo, from Euphorbos and from Hector. This tripartite killing is what I would argue is akin to the sacrificial gesture during which a victim is immolated; one can see this in Scroll iii of the Homeric Odyssey, where old King Nestor commissions a formal ceremony during which a bovine victim is felled, again, with three exacting blows. In the classical drama by Aeschylus where Queen Clytemnestra murders her husband Agamemnon, she does this by means of three similar hits and later describes the moment in terms of a joyous instant of ritual fertility and harmony.[56] The point is that epic heroes die in a manner that is metaphorically an instant of translation towards a situation that is more-than-mortal and therefore close to a divine condition; I would particularly cite the death of Karṇa here, as evinced by the poets. Saṃjaya tells of his last minute as follows:

54 Il.XVI, 705, for instance.

55 Such an instantaneous and ultimate circumstance is akin to the brief moment of erotic union as presented in poem Thirty-One of Sappho: both epiphanic moments are equated with being *like* a divine union that is overwhelmingly deathly.

56 Ag. 1386.

VIII,67,27: *dehāt tu karṇasya nipātitasya*
tejo dīptaṃ khaṃ vigāhyācireṇa.
From the body of the felled Karṇa
Splendour, plunging quickly into the sky, blazed.

I have elsewhere written at length about the presence of death in these epics and about how, living and dying on the margin of existence, heroes dramatize and make real that boundary between the cosmos and the sub-lunar world.[57]

Yet curiously, in both the Homeric Iliad and in the *Great Bhārata* there is never any mention of pain or horror, certainly not as occurs in modern cinema where death, violence and corporeal trauma are both visually and acoustically most explicit. Death in this late Bronze Age poetry is made beautiful and lovely and presented in terms of wonderful metaphor and simile; it is never horrible, repulsive or ghastly, and certainly bodily pain is never depicted despite there being so much traumatic combat at work. For example, there is the martial passion of Bhīṣma as he approaches death:

VI,114,5: *sa dīptaśaracāpārcir astraprasṛtamārutaḥ*
neminirhrādasaṃnādo mahāstrodayapāvakaḥ
citracāpamahājvālo vīrakṣayamahendhanaḥ
yugāntāgnisamo bhīṣmaḥ pareṣāṃ samapadyata
He, Bhīṣma, became among enemies like the fire at the end of a yuga:
The fire – bow and arrows blazing, the wind – the discharged missiles,
The clamour of the roar of wheel-fellies – the flame of uprisen great missiles,
The beautiful bow – a great flame, the destruction of warriors – A huge kindling …

What happens during these moments of armed contention and physical mortality is that the frontier between the timeless world of the universe, where the deities reside, and the temporal and human world of the heroes is made overt in the poetry.

That is, where death is being so stylized and depicted, so visually dramatized and particularly in terms of metaphor, that moment, that instant,

57 McGrath, 2018b, ch. 6.

is what I would argue is simultaneously mirroring and designating the origin of human consciousness. This is the palpable charge of epic poetry as it functions socially and ritually. In contemporary cinema death is permanent, whereas in these epics death is transitory and lovely, an instant where the mortal merges with the immortal and undying, an occasion that is forever to be recalled in song and perhaps reactivated in later rites and cult ceremonies. In the Svargārohaṇa *parvan* of the *Great Bhārata*, the audience actually witness the deceased warriors 'living' on after their death.

Through the literal contiguity in the demise of mortal heroes and the immediate living presence of immortal deities, the division between the timely and the timeless is thus staged: this is the ground of epic poetry, where death is a terrible and always present margin or frontier upon which the narrative occurs. On the one side there are the mortal heroes who die and on the other side are the immortal deities who receive the deceased heroes, and it is this strangely infinite and median world which the epic poetry of Vyāsa expresses, represents and dominates.

In the two Homeric poems only the audience as well as Achilles actually perceive the deities and hear their words during the Iliad song, and in his poem Odysseus only *sees* Athena in her many disguises, never as an actual deity, but the audience does. Within the *Great Bhārata* divinities are overt and participate in the action of the plot and story: the Greek audience does not experience such cognitive intimacy and hence what is being accomplished by the narrative is different – which is our next point.

Finally, there is one crucial distinction between these two ancient epics, for nowhere does the Homeric Iliad proclaim the moral efficacy of its performance. This is something that the *Great Bhārata* iterates and reiterates, in the beginning of the poem during the Ādi *parvan* and at the end of the Song during the Svargārohaṇa *parvan*. That is, the participation of an audience at the performance of the *Mahābhārata* as well as the sponsoring of the poem's production are spiritually and morally efficient. For instance, the poets say,

> XVIII,5,51: *imāṃ bhāratasāvitrīṃ prātar utthāya yaḥ paṭhet*
> *sa bhārataphalaṃ prāpya paraṃ brahmādhigacchati*
> Whoever rehearses this Bhārata Song, having risen at dawn,
> He, having obtained the reward of the Bhārata, proceeds toward the ultimate Brahma.[58]

---

58 In the Bombay Edition of the poem, the final *adhyāya* of the epic is referred to as *mahābhārataśravaṇamahimā*, 'the greatness come of the hearing of the Great Bhārata'.

Many are the occasions, at the commencement and conclusion of the epic, when this sentiment or *phalastuti* is declaimed.

As a *coda* to all the above, Homeric poetry, like all of the European epic song traditions, is presently long *frozen* in time and has ceased to exist as a dynamic component of contemporary Greek culture and society. This is of course completely unlike the *Great Bhārata*, which exists today as a vivid and lively presence in modern Indian life: as poetry and prose, in the cinema and on television, and in other artistic media, and even in national political life. Heroes and heroines are no longer worshipped in Greece, the veneration of Achilles and of Helen exists no more, whereas in contemporary South Asia, Arjuna and Kṛṣṇa, Draupadī, Karṇa and Bhīṣma, to name a few epic characters, continue to receive much ritual devotion at certain festal times of the year. These ritual places where the epic heroes and heroines receive adoration are of course founded upon their initial appearance and life in the *Great Bhārata* of Vyāsa. In Chapter 6, we partially revisit this point.

In sum, then, the above are a few aspects that illustrate and represent the vast and ancient kinship which exists between these two most beautiful and near perfect epic songs.[59] It is the cognate quality of the two poetic traditions which allows us to reflect upon the performative and substantial nature of their poetry: by examining one tradition the other poem can be conceptually illuminated, and vice versa. This kind of intellectual activity is central to our work as professional humanists, who in our attempts to comprehend *what we are not* come to terms with the magnificent and wonderful presence of what we might actually possess.

In conclusion, I would argue that Vyāsa's *Great Bhārata* has been a source of political legitimacy for centuries, beginning with the Gupta hegemony, and also the literary origins of what we now consider to be Classical Hinduism. Nowadays, not only is the narrative of the *Great Bhārata* employed by contemporary Indian politicians, film directors and novelists, but likewise, Vyāsa – *or the poets who created Vyāsa* and the logistics of the poem's inspiration – has drawn upon a most ancient Āryan tradition of poetry in order to compose this epic. It is the intellectual, ritual and historical mastery of the figure of Vyāsa which, having reproduced certain ancient threads of the Āryan poetic tradition, infused those strands into a geopolitical drama which possessed such inherent truth and literary dynamism that the song continues into the

---

This consists of 105 *ślokas* devoted to and describing in precise detail the spiritual and diurnal benefits of attending to the performance of the epic.

59 In her magisterial work, a scholar like Bachvarova, 2016, p. 4, concerning other possible sources for the Homeric system of epic poetry, would assert that 'Hurro-Hittite narrative poetry, attested almost exclusively in the Hittite archives […] presents a

twenty-first century, sustaining and expressing those profoundly conceptual strains of Indian culture.

Likewise, to demonstrate how such ancient Indian sentiments might have functioned, in his modern mimesis a writer like Shashi Tharoor would even go so far as to say that the *Great Bhārata* is the *charter myth* of modern and contemporary India, insofar as this is the primary lore which coheres and transmits much of contemporary Indic understanding of human value and worth as well as a specific social or moral taxonomy.[60] To reiterate an earlier point, human culture is never unique in time but is always driven by past events, experience and record; this is as true today as it was three thousand years ago when *ṛṣi* Vyāsa was composing, or when he was 'being composed' by the poets of that era. It is in this fashion that poetry becomes the *genius* of a culture and is constantly being renewed and reformed as it moves through time.

As a contemporary example of such kinds of mimesis, allow me to quote from the end of Martin West's compendious study of Āryan heroic poetry traditions.[61] In his 'Elegy' at the close of the work he imitates the tradition as he has learned it, being inspired not visually or acoustically but through a scholarly life of close *reading* the texts of many late Bronze Age epics.[62] Through his encyclopaedic learning he was able to reproduce – yet in an original fashion – an invented model or copy of how those poetic conventions and literary customs had once functioned. Let me quote the first two stanzas as an example: 'Urukleves now I call to mind, / the son of valiant Seghekleves, / who with his great thirsty spear / slew men and horses by hundreds. // Many a day he arose with the sun / and led the war-host to the field of blood: / there they fought like raging fire, / army against army, man against man.'

In a similar manner of multitextual simulation, Tolkien with his *Lord of the Rings*, thanks to his prodigious erudition, was able to produce his own prose epic which drew upon Germanic and Old English tradition.[63] In his life's work Tolkien was also able to create his own maps and geography and even his own alphabet as he innovatively copied yet *renewed* the style and themes of a much earlier kind of composition. It is remarkable that inspiration in this case

---

precious witness for the prehistory of the Homeric tradition.' That is, no *tradition* is unique; there are no entities but only continuities in this kind of ancient culture of epic poetry.

60 Tharoor, personal communication, 2006.

61 West, 2007, p. 504.

62 Kerrigan, 2018, has demonstrated how the extremely literate William Shakespeare drew upon earlier texts – in English and in translations from the Latin – for many of his plots, scenes and even at times vocabulary and metaphors.

63 Tolkien, 1954–55. The author incorporated thematic elements and motifs from the *Nibelungenlied*, the *Beowulf*, the Norse *Sagas* and *Eddas*, and other like works.

derived from familiarity with the tradition *via* its written media and that *experience* in this case was far removed – both historically and sensibly – from the far-off ancient events that once impelled the poets to sing. Curiously, Tolkien's character of Gandalf is akin to the figure of Vyāsa, insofar as both *maestros* are able to comprehend both past and future and magically direct the movement and development of the present.

Let us close this chapter with another quote from Nair's modernist *Echoes from the Mahabharata*, where she describes the birth of Vyāsa, imitating and copying whilst she simultaneously innovates: 'Painlessly – oh, the only time – and quick as a chime did the child arrive, full-grown and – sadly – pedantic. He named himself Ved Vyaasa, river of the sacred scripts, bowed, then vanished in his ascetic father's footsteps, leaving me with the aftertaste of victory, the sweet odour of eternity.'[64]

---

64 Nair, 2015, p. 24.

Chapter 4

VYĀSA

Kṛṣṇa Dvaipāyana is initially mentioned by the poet Ugraśravas as being the one who first made a declaration of the poem – part of which constitutes the *Great Bhārata* as we know it today – which was then recited by Vaiśaṃpāyana; we analysed this sequence in Chapter 2. Now, in this present chapter, let us examine how Vyāsa is portrayed by the poets during the period before *and* after the battle at Kurukṣetra, that is, how he appears as a *character* in the central area of the poem. Let us also look at how he is described during that conflict and, then, how he appears after the fighting has ended, for in the latter instance his personality becomes markedly changed.

The *ṛṣi* is actually introduced into the poem with the title Kṛṣṇa Dvaipāyana; in fact, this is how he is referred to during the beginning of the Ādi *parvan*, for he is only named as Vyāsa in the second *adhyāya* or 'chapter'. He is called *dvaipāyana* as he was born on a *dvīpa*, 'island', in the Yamunā (I,57,71). He is also often referred to as *satyavatīsuta*, 'the son of Satyavatī', and as *parāśarātmajo*, 'the son of Parāśara' (I,1,52–53). Vyāsa is said to be descended from Vedic *ṛṣi* Vasiṣṭha, who was his paternal great-great-grandfather.[1] His mother, Satyavatī, had been born from a fish and her twin brother became the founding king of the Mātsya people (I,54,2 and I,57,32–75). A princess of this clan is later married to Abhimanyu, the son of Arjuna, and their child is the future successor who rules at Hāstinapura after the war at Kurukṣetra and whose own son is the patron of the epic. Thus Vyāsa does possess some slight genetic connection with *rāja* Janamejaya through the matriline, Janamejaya being a distant cousin to the *ṛṣi*.

This progeny of Satyavatī and Parāśara was called Kṛṣṇa, *kārṣṇyātvāt*, 'due to his darkness' (I,99,14). Later, as he was reputedly the figure to organize the division of the Vedas – *vivyāsa vedān*, 'he separated the Vedas' – he became known as Vedavyāsa, abbreviated to Vyāsa (I,57,73); the *Mahābhārata* by this account is considered to be the 'Fifth Veda'. The cosmogony, style and

1 In terms of 'textual' time, this would be in the late third millennium BC.

reservoir of belief in the *Great Bhārata* have little in common with any Vedic poetry, however.

It is notable that the lineage which directly descends from Vyāsa as it appears in the poem is begun by the virgin progenitrix – Satyavatī – whose name means 'the one who possesses truth'. This lineage, of course, only concerns the Dhārtarāṣṭras, *not* the Pāṇḍavas, for Vyāsa has a genetic connection only with the former moiety of the clan – they are his grandsons – whereas with the Pāṇḍava half-brothers his interest is primarily political and possibly spiritual, but not biological. By virtue of the fact that it is the Yādava clan – as I argued in the previous chapter – who are the political community to triumph after the great battle at Kurukṣetra, Vyāsa must be somehow affiliated with that kin group of Kṛṣṇa Vāsudeva. This, I would contend, comes not from reasons of poetic inspiration but from those of textual edition, a point that was proposed earlier, in the second chapter.

In the beginning, Ugraśravas says that he heard,

> I,1,9: *kṛṣṇadvaipāyanaproktāḥ supuṇyā vividhāḥ kathāḥ*
> *kathitāś cāpi vidhivadyā vaiśaṃpāyanena vai*
> The epic, auspicious, various, proclaimed by Kṛṣṇa Dvaipāyana
> And then told by Vaiśaṃpāyana accordingly.

As we know, it is the declamation of Vaiśaṃpāyana which Ugraśravas hears, that is, he is third in the line of transmission, and this occurred at the snake sacrifice of Janamejaya.[2] At that rite Ugraśravas says that Vyāsa held the position of *sadasya*, 'the priest who observes any instance of ceremonial error', yet it is unclear how Vyāsa would have performed this role whilst simultaneously delivering the original poetry (I,48,7). Let us return to this point later.

The whole poem closes with Janamejaya departing from Takṣaśilā, where this rite had been performed and where the epic had been initially pronounced (XVIII,5,29); thus, what Ugraśravas is reciting is what he heard there, in present-day Afghanistan. The end of that rite thus becomes the conclusion of the epic poem which Ugraśravas reports and declaims much later in the Naimiṣa forest, and so the poem as we have it now becomes something of a circumference in that it circles back to its origin.[3] Thus there are three places involved in the

2 It is later stated that Vyāsa also taught Sumantu, Jaimini, Phaila and his own son Śuka (I,57,74).

3 Ring composition, where a narrative concludes at the same point as it began, is common in preliterate poetry. The narrative of modern detective fiction demonstrates a similar organization of time and causality: for the detective, in his or her pursuit of the criminal

Great Bhārata's overall narrative performance: the ritual which is occurring in Takṣaśilā, the contention and war in Bhāratavarṣa, and the Naimiṣa forest narration. All these converge simultaneously as the poem moves forward and backwards in reported time, Vyāsa being hypothetically present only during the former two performances. Naimiṣa, where the poem commences, is actually the last point in time which occurs in this sequence, although our present text begins at that *venue*; the poem concludes with what was in fact the historically originating moment of the sequence. This paradox presents a logical predicament to the close reader, yet it is typical of how Vyāsa's presence is profoundly polytropic.

It is said that when Dhṛtarāṣṭra, Pāṇḍu and Vidura had expired, Vyāsa then delivered the *Bhārata* to humanity: *abravīt bhāratam̥ loke mānuṣe'smin*, 'he spoke the Bhārata in this mortal world' (I,1,56). He, then, *śaśāsa śiṣyam [...] vaiśam̥pāyanam*, 'taught his student Vaiśam̥pāyana'. This *Bhārata* is described as containing:

> I,1,59: *vistaram̥ kuruvaṅśasya gāndhārya dharmaśīlatām*
> *kṣattuḥ prajñām̥ dhṛtim̥ kuntyāḥ samyag dvaipāyano'bravīt*
> *vāsudevasya māhātmyam̥ pāṇḍavānām̥ ca satyatām*
> *durvṛittam̥ dhārtarāṣṭrāṇām̥ uktavān bhagavān ṛṣiḥ*
> Dvaipāyana told entirely the extent of the Kuru lineage, Gāndhārī's skill in *dharma*,
> The wisdom of the steward, Kuntī's fortitude;
> The lordly *ṛṣi* declared the greatness of Vāsudeva, and the veracity of the Pāṇḍavas,
> The bad conduct of the Dhārtarāṣṭras.

This is how the *Bhārata* of 24,000 verses was constituted. During the course of the Ādi *parvan* the textual distinction between the *Bhārata*, the *Jaya* and the *Mahābhārata* is never precise, and these terms possess the uncertain and labile quality of synonymy.[4] I would in fact argue that this kind of textual dubiety is intentional and purposefully irrational insofar as it conduces to a poem that

who accomplished the crime which generated the narration of the book, completes a series of metonymical connections which lead him or her *back* to that original moment when the crime was performed. That instant of lucid realization as to who was the originating perpetrator occurs at the end of the book, thus simulating what we might consider as a mode of ring composition.

4 For instance, such a moment of synonymity occurs at I,1,208–9, where the poem is both *Bhārata* and *Mahābhārata*. For the *anukramaṇī*, the poem is referred to as the *Bhārata* (I,2,29) and then for the *parvasam̥graha* it is also called the *Bhārata* (I,2,71). In the *mahābhārataśravanamahīmā*, 'the consequence of hearing the Great Bhārata', which is the final *adhyāya* in the Bombay Edition of the poem, the epic is likewise referred to as the *Bhārata*.

cannot be logically disassembled; this Bhārata poem is referred to as a *kathā*, 'epic' (I,53,28 and 31). It is declared that:

I,53,33: *śrāvayāmāsa vidivat tadā karmāntareṣu saḥ*
Then he declaimed this appropriately during the pauses in the rite.

At this point in the poem Vyāsa is said to be a *brahmarṣiḥ kaviḥ*, 'a holy sage-poet' or 'prophet' (I,54,5).

Ugraśravas says that Janamejaya commissions Vyāsa with the statement,

I,54,18: *kurūṇāṃ pāṇḍavānāṃ ca bhavān pratyakṣadarṣivān*
teṣāṃ caritam icchāmi kathyamānaṃ tvayā dvija
kathaṃ samabhavad bhedas teṣām akliṣṭakarmaṇām
tac ca yuddhaṃ kathaṃ vṛittaṃ bhūtāntakaraṇaṃ mahat
You, sir, witnessed the legend of those Kurus and Pāṇḍavas,
O twice-born, I wish to be told by you …
How the partition arose among those of tireless action,
And about the war and how the great conclusive event occurred.

As we demonstrated earlier, this is how the poet is directed, but Vyāsa, however, does not respond to this in person but instructs his loyal student, Vaiśaṃpāyana, to deliver the *kathā*, 'the song'. Thus that first *idealized* telling is occluded, for there is a strangely vague *ellipsis* occurring here due to that initial Bhārata *not* being delivered, and instead there is the retelling which Vaiśaṃpāyana recites (I,54,21–24). The commission, by both king and Vyāsa, is to tell of *bheda*, 'the partition', nothing else, and this is given in precise summary form in 37 *ślokas*, describing the rivalry between the young cousins, the marriage to Draupadī, their lives in the Khāṇḍava forest, the gambling – although no mention is made of the *rājasūya* ceremony – the subsequent long exile and then the war (I,55,6–43).

As we have already seen, this is said to be the *Great Bhārata* and to contain a hundred thousand *ślokas* (I,56,1 and 13), yet it is also said to be the *Bhārata* and to be called the *Jaya*; such is the play of synonymy (I,56,19 and 27). Vaiśaṃpāyana says that Vyāsa accomplished the former telling of this poem during the course of three years (I,56,32). This blurring of events during the narrative is not uncommon in the poem, and it is this which brings to the work an arbitrary and super-tensile quality; there are no obvious evident errors though, and hence the poem possesses an implausible nature, something akin to a Möbius band which appears to own only one topological side when represented in Euclidean dimension.

When Vyāsa is born – and it is as if he immediately becomes adult – he promises to his mother, *smṛto'haṃ darśayiṣyāmi*, 'remembered [by you], I shall appear' (I,57,70). These words mark his physical and vocal entry into the poem and this is his preliminary first-person utterance, which means that Satyavatī will be able to summon Vyāsa whenever she wishes, as when he is needed to procreate with her daughters-in-law (I,90,56). This moment also marks the first occasion when he demonstrates his telepathic and visionary capacities; telepathy, as we remarked earlier, is an ability which one of the other male Kṛṣṇas in the poem – Kṛṣṇa Vāsudeva – also possesses.

By the admonition of his mother, Satyavatī, Vyāsa is encouraged to inseminate her two widowed daughters-in-law in order that the lineage might proceed and not become defunct; the daughters-in-law are from Kāśi, modern Vārāṇasī. This he accomplishes and Dhṛtarāṣṭra is the firstborn, followed by Pāṇḍu and then Vidura, the latter being born of a servant woman (I,100,27). Thus the audience perceive Vyāsa taking an actively causal role in the poem where his actions generate the movement of plot by causing the birth of the future leaders of the clan moieties. He is not simply poet-creator of the work but he also participates in that work as a character who possesses significant personal agency; that is, he possesses a double complexion of causality.

Then, for the subsequent generation, when Gāndhārī – his own daughter-in-law – was once kind to Vyāsa, he offered to please her with a gift: she asked for a hundred sons (I,107,7–8). He then magically facilitated their actual parturition when problems occurred after Gāndhārī had caused her embryos to become aborted (I,107,11–34).

Soon, when Pāṇḍu – one of the sons born of a Kāśi woman – dies and is cremated, Vyāsa sends Satyavatī off towards the forest, warning her that great suffering and disorder are soon to be prevalent in the world. He says,

> I,119,6: *atikrāntasukhāḥ kālāḥ pratyupasthitadāruṇāḥ*
> The happy days are exceeded, dreadful ones approach.

This is the second occasion in the poem where the *ṛṣi* demonstrates the supernatural quality of his mind, and it is now that Vyāsa becomes closer to the Pāṇḍava half-brothers, when he realizes that the flamboyant Duryodhana and his male siblings are pursuing a disastrous political course. This is a significant point in the epic narrative, for it is now that the *ṛṣi* moves his fidelity from the Dhārtarāṣṭras towards the Pāṇḍavas; let us recall that he is the genetic grandfather of the former but not of the latter.

Paradoxically, however, as Vyāsa is the causal voice of the *Bhārata*, this calamitous division between clan moieties is of his own original creation. Or, is it that Vyāsa's first poem, the *Jaya*, is a historical record of what had actually happened in earthly and chronological time?[5]

These are the three likely scenarios: a possible historical event that is recounted, the original poem of Vyāsa and the epic in which Vyāsa is a character of dramatic efficiency. It is impossible to separate these perspectives, yet the dimensions remain forever convergent. For me this is essentially the irreducible beauty of the poem's perfectly composite narration.

Such is a curious shift – from loyalty to the Dhārtarāṣṭras to adherence to the Pāṇḍavas – for the poem's narrative force usually emphasizes the priority of genetic series over that of mere affiliation: suddenly that model of biological faith is abandoned. One wonders if this moment was not an instance of edition in which those Bhārgava editors merged the presence of Vyāsa with that of Yādava influence on the epic. Vyāsa says,

> I,144,7: *mayedaṃ manasā pūrvaṃ viditaṃ bharatarṣabhāḥ*
> *yathā sthitair adharmeṇa dhārtarāṣṭrair vivāsitāḥ*
> This, [was] once known mentally by me, O Bhārata bulls,
> How [you] were expelled by the non-dharmic Dhārtarāṣṭras.

This is of course one more occasion when the *ṛṣi* reveals the knowledge which he possesses due to especial powers of intellectual foresight, and he confesses, *tasmād abhyadhikaḥ sneho yuṣmāsu*, 'therefore my love is excessive for you' (I,144,10). This is a vital instant in the narrative progress indicating a new and most explicit devotion which Vyāsa has for the half-brothers whilst he simultaneously spurns his direct descendants: in this sense, affiliation has suddenly become more important than bloodline in the *Great Bhārata*. Let us remember that these Pāṇḍava youths have not yet met Kṛṣṇa Vāsudeva or made any alliance with the Yādava clan.

However, as we noted earlier, let us also recall that through his maternal uncle, the twin of his mother Satyavatī, called Matsya, a lineage was generated into which Abhimanyu, the son of Arjuna, is later to marry, and from that union Parikṣit will be born, the father of Janamejaya. Thus Satyavatī's genetic presence, and hence of course that of Vyāsa, is actually participating in that future Bhārata ruler, conjoined with Yādava blood: such is the biological

5 The *Bhārata* might possibly have been a bygone record, but the *Great Bhārata*, with all the genealogical, didactic, mythological and cosmogonic descriptions, cannot be considered as a historical document. One simple reason is that the material culture portrayed – as we remarked in Chapter 3 – is too historically diverse.

conformation or inheritance of Janamejaya, one that has descended from the maternal side.[6]

To Kuntī – his other daughter-in-law – Vyāsa predicts, *sutas te'yaṃ dharmaputro yudhiṣṭhiraḥ*, 'this, your son Yudhiṣṭhira is the Son of *Dharma*', and *praśāsiṣyati dharmarāṭ*, 'as *Dharma* King he shall rule' (I,144,13). The statement indicates how Vyāsa, once again, possesses the mental acuity to *know* that Yudhiṣṭhira's father is the deity Dharma. Thus the audience become increasingly aware of how Vyāsa, through his extra-cognitive skill of forecast, is increasingly directing the narrative, not by poetic composition or by actual material causation but by prophetic speech acts.[7] He controls the narrative by literal *prediction*, for what he says does happen, that is, he is dominating the *plot*. He creates the original poem, that founding speech act; he is biologically involved with the two competing sides of the ruling clan; and he constantly influences the plot with his words of either direct causality or prognostication.

Vyāsa does this in such a manner, however, that it seems that he merely foresees events rather than causing them to occur mentally; the distinction is important and yet it is effectively conjoint, for the two roles of poet-creator of the narrative and actor-character within that poem are now inseparably compounded. Again, this is an occasioning of an impossible situation, but one that is accomplished in such a manner as to be dramatically effective and also wonderful. In the Āraṇyaka *parvan* there is mention of Vyāsa perceiving events which occur far away: *dṛṣṭvā divyena cakṣuṣā*, 'having witnessed by divine vision', the poets say (III,8,22). It is this supernatural ability which, as we have noted earlier, he transmits to Saṃjaya so that the poet might truly visualize the events of battle at Kurukṣetra.[8]

Vyāsa is thus polytropic and multitudinous in terms of how he is present both within and without the Bhārata Song; it is as if, via all these varying kinds of presence and perception with which he supplies the elan and charges the movement of the work – creatively, verbally, through foresight and also by offering emotional sustenance at times – that Vyāsa is the master of *all* sequence in the work, regardless of temporal moment. No other character in the poem is so practically multiplex and dramatically puissant in terms of

6 As we noted in the previous chapter, the Yādavas practised matrilineal kinship relations. See also McGrath, 2017a.

7 For the nature of speech acts, see Austin, 1962; and Searle, 1969. Unlike other kinds of statement, a speech act is neither true nor false but is simply effective or non-effective.

8 Again, this is to presume that there was a historical event and that Vyāsa or the poets who created Vyāsa were not creating a completely fictional narrative. Such is the nature of *myth*, where truth is not an empirical reality but merely a unique and morally fruitful recollection, one that has significant meaning.

causing how the narrative moves. In fact, I know of no such fulfilling character in epic literature, except perhaps Athena in the Homeric Odyssey.

Vyāsa then, in his words to Kuntī, predicts the imperial success of Yudhiṣṭhira:

> I,144,16: *yakṣyanti ca naravyāghrā vijitya prithivīm imām*
> *rājasūyāśvamedhādyaiḥ kratubhir bhūridakṣiṇaiḥ*
> The tigers of men having conquered this entire earth will sacrifice
> With the *rājasūya* and *aśvamedha* and other affluent rites.

In this same manner, Vyāsa later appears to the young warriors and informs them about Kṛṣṇā or Draupadī and he tells them, *nirdiṣṭā bhavatāṃ patnī*, 'of you she is the destined wife' (I,157,14). Again, the audience perceives how Vyāsa directs the movement of the narrative with his predictions, which are in fact admonitions, and hence the half-brothers set off to win this woman.[9] They acquire her as a wife who is shared among themselves, and once the nuptials are performed they then set off towards the Khāṇḍava forest where Vyāsa again appears and assists in the planning of their Indraprastha citadel (I,199,27).

Now, not long before this visit by Vyāsa, the *ṛṣi* had spoken to Yudhiṣṭhira in a private fashion. This heralds something that is unusual in the poem and reveals another aspect of how the seer both communicates and works *within* the narrative, for here it is as if Vyāsa is initiating the young prince into esoteric teaching. He says,

> I,188,18: *na tu vakṣyāmi sarveṣāṃ pāñcāla śṛṇu me svayam*
> For I shall not speak among all, O Pāñcāla, hear this from me yourself.

It is curious that Vyāsa here addresses the prince as Pāñcāla, something which he is not, except by marital affiliation. To my present knowledge Vyāsa never does this again in the poem. Vaiśaṃpāyana then says that Vyāsa,

---

9 Let us recall that Draupadī is not actually mortal, being born from a ritual hearth and fire and *not* from human parents (I,175,7). In fact, of the four figures in the poem who receive the title of *kṛṣṇa/ā* – that is, Vyāsa, Draupadī, Hṛśikeṣa Vāsudeva and Arjuna, the latter two being at times referred to as *dvau kṛṣṇau* – only heroic Kṛṣṇa Vāsudeva is born of two mortal parents. This is ironic as he is the only one of the group to become a divinity, one who is later to be fully worshipped.

I,188,20: *kare gṛhītvā rājānaṃ rājaveśma samāviśat*
Having taken the king's hand he entered the royal quarter.[10]

This marks the beginning of a secret discourse between king and prophet, a form of relation that recurs throughout the poem. It is rare in this kind of epic narrative for dialogue to be given as exclusive and undisclosed, for such cannot obviously have effect on the plot. It is remarkable that the poets actually engage with this kind of discreet conversation, and the fact that the exchange is referred to during successive moments in the epic is revealing of a certain and most specific yet opaque intention.

Vyāsa drifts in and out of the narrative, casually appearing and sometimes speaking, as at III,13,99 and III,91,17.[11] It is curious as to how he suddenly presents himself, or how the poets indicate him, sometimes with simply a casual reference, at other times with significant influence on how the plot is developing. On one of these latter occasions, whilst the Pāṇḍava half-brothers are in exile he arrives without notice and speaks with Yudhiṣṭhira, saying, *vedmi te hṛdi mānasam*, 'I know the thought in your heart' (III,37,22). This is evidence of his telepathic ability once again, and he says,

III,37,27: *gṛhāṇemāṃ mayā proktāṃ siddhiṃ mūrtimatīm iva*
Take this learning spoken by me, as if corporeal.

He then imparts directions which the king is to relay to his half-brother, Arjuna, the great warrior, about how Arjuna is to journey towards Indra, Rudra and Varuṇa, in order to obtain supernatural missiles. The *ṛṣi* now again speaks privately with Yudhiṣṭhira, *ekāntam unnīya*, 'having led him apart', and the poets say that Vyāsa on that occasion pronounced *yogavidyām anuttamām*, 'the ultimate knowledge of *yoga*' (III,37,34). He then proceeds to initiate the king into this *vidyā*, 'magic', informing him as to how Yudhiṣṭhira must instruct Arjuna so that the latter becomes able to acquire celestial and supernatural weaponry.

10 Remember that Vaiśaṃpāyana is here repeating verbatim what he had ostensibly heard Vyāsa declaim at the initial performance of the *Bhārata*: a paradox.

11 III,245,8 to 247,46 is another occasion when Vyāsa simply appears in the narrative, this time to deliver a hortatory oration on *tapas*, 'severe meditation'; the speech develops into an edifying micronarrative about Mudgala. This event which occurs between *rāja* Yudhiṣṭhira and Vyāsa has no import upon the plot and is simply another instructive moment of discourse typical of the Āraṇyaka *parvan*. At V,65,8 during Saṃjaya's embassy to the Hāstinapura court, Vyāsa once more suddenly emerges into the narrative, and at V,67,11 he admonishes Dhṛtarāṣṭra towards a policy of peace-making; on this occasion his words remain feckless.

Without this armoury which Arjuna successfully acquires, the Pāṇḍavas would not have been able to win at Kurukṣetra, not against such paramount and superhuman heroes as Bhīṣma and Karṇa. Once again the audience perceives how the *ṛṣi* dominates and leads the plot, and in this particular case he predicts the victory of Arjuna against his enemies. Concerning this initiation the poets say,

> III,37,36: *yudhiṣṭhiras tu dharmātmā tad brahma manasā yataḥ*
> *dhārayāmāsa medhāvī kāle kāle samabhyasan*
> Yudhiṣṭhira the dharmic one retained that sacred speech thoughtfully,
> He bore it intelligently, practising again and again.

Thus the audience perceive not only how Saṃjaya has been initiated into esoteric knowledge, along with Bhīṣma, but that the king himself is so unspeakably involved in this assessment of mystery. Yudhiṣṭhira communicates the learning to Arjuna, who then proceeds on his long journey towards the deities in order to acquire the desired martial skills; the ruthless and pugnacious Arjuna is the only hero in the poem to make such supernatural travels.

As we have said, the vital point about these plot-oriented interventions by the poet, however, is not simply that Vyāsa is a director of the narrative *qua* actor or character in the poem, but that he also is the one who is said to have verbally originated the poem in which these personal events occur. Likewise, when describing his troubled experience of the *rājasūya*, Duryodhana tells of how Vyāsa, along with Yudhiṣṭhira's personal *purohita* or 'chaplain' Dhaumya, performed the actual coronal anointment of the king, the *abhiṣeka* (II,49,10).

Vyāsa is hence placing himself within the narrative at the same time as he performs the words; or, the poets and editors are doing this, so creating an illusion of Vyāsa's originality. Saṃjaya, the inner poet of the song, as we have already observed, also possesses the *divyaṃ cakṣur*, 'divine vision', when he performs the four Kurukṣetra Books, for at times he occasionally places himself within the narrative as a character. It is as if the persona of a playwright were to appear within the poetic or dramatic works, and this is just another aspect of the uniquely incongruous quality of *Great Bhārata* poetics which are so logically baffling.[12]

The *ṛṣi* Nārada also intervenes in the poem and tells of events that are about to occur in the future and of events that occurred long ago in the past

---

12 Both Virgil and Shakespeare were putatively telling of empirical historical events which they proceeded to fictionalize; they were both producing foundation myths for their respective patron regimes, the lineage of Augustus and the house of Tudor.

which influence what happens in the present. Nārada is not a poet, though, and has no biological investment with the clan.[13]

Much later, towards the close of the poem and when *rāja* Yudhiṣṭhira is present in the forest at the mysterious death of Vidura, the poets reiterate this point about confidential and mysterious communication, reminding the audience about the intellectual insight which had once been transmitted. They say of Yudhiṣṭhira that he was

> XV,33,29: *yogadharmaṃ mahātejā vyāsena kathitaṃ yathā*
> The spiritually bright one, as once instructed in dharmic *yoga* by Vyāsa.

There is thus an undisclosed discourse which occurs throughout the poem between these two – king and *ṛṣi* – and it is a manner of communication that is restricted and unmatched in the epic and strangely rare; no other character makes this kind of limited election. As we noted earlier, on other such occasions – as when heroic Kṛṣṇa initiates Bhīṣma and Vidura in the Sabhā *parvan* and then, later, Arjuna during the Bhīṣma *parvan*, or when Vyāsa himself supplies Saṃjaya with an especial telepathic vision – this is made thoroughly explicit. Such is not the case with what happens between *rāja* and poet. This kind of discreet and undemonstrated communication is deeply uncharacteristic of the other Āryan epic systems – like the Homeric – which we have also been discussing and which we shall briefly return to at the close of this book.[14]

Let us quickly rehearse the narrative model which is being activated and engaged here and make overt how it is actually being staged, for at this point one must remember that all this is being declaimed by Vaiśaṃpāyana, who is reciting what he had *heard* from his *guru* on an earlier occasion: that is, the poet is telling *rāja* Janamejaya about his great-grandfather and great-great-uncles and about what he once heard Vyāsa perform concerning events three generations prior to that moment. This in itself is being reperformed by Ugraśravas, who lived a generation after Vaiśaṃpāyana. There is also a further disjunction in that the poet who reports the words of Ugraśravas

---

13 In McGrath, 2016, ch. 6, I outlined and analysed the presence of Nārada in the *Great Bhārata*.

14 When the deity Athena speaks with Achilles at I,100, we the audience are able to perceive and apprehend the communication although the figures in the poem are themselves unaware of the exchange. In a like vein, Privitera, 2015, has closely read both the Homeric epics and analysed non-verbal communication and perception and how characters within a narrative become aware of the thought and affect of other characters. This is different from *discreet* or private spoken communication, however.

himself lives *after* that poet's time; yet, as we noted earlier, this anonymous master poet only proclaims the first nine *ślokas* of the work and a few other momentary *ślokas*, before that second master voice intervenes and continues the poem.

To revisit what we observed earlier in Chapter 2, the principal poem concerns Vyāsa's song where he tells of the ancestral past, and it is given at the snake sacrifice of *rāja* Janamejaya. This is in the voice of Vaiśaṃpāyana, who is recalling what his *guru* proclaimed on an earlier and unspecified occasion – the unidentified and unspecified *ur*-moment or the *zero*-time – which in its turn is being repeated long afterwards in the Naimiṣa forest by Ugraśravas, and then by someone else who is absolutely nameless and placeless.

To summarize, in this great poem Vyāsa is the primary creator; he is also an agent or character in the poem who directs the narrative with his words that generate an ongoing and impulsive metonymy; and he is this strangely secret communicator who apparently influences – as an active manager within the poem itself – how the plot moves. This simultaneous combination of narrative dimensions is truly remarkable.[15]

It is said that during the plenipotential *rājasūya* rite of Yudhiṣṭhira, among all the various priests who officiate, Vyāsa performs the role of the *brahmán*, that is, he is the most important official at the ritual, one who oversees all *praxis*. In fact, Vyāsa can also be said to perform this role for the performance of the whole poem, if one can consider the poetry and its expression a rite: for he is the one to appear and comment when there is need for direction.

Despite all this magical appearing and disappearing and his supernatural cognition that allows him to foresee and predict future events, Vyāsa always remains a *brāhmaṇa*, a priest who is completely competent in all the ancient Vedic ceremonies. Hence his hieratic role of supplying and administering private and undisclosed information is not so incongruous after all but suits this ancient position of ritual officer. We discussed – at the end of Chapter 3 – how the poem partakes of a ritual form and that the poetry itself actually and demonstratively proclaims this. Such an interpretation, however, in which the performance of the poem reflects the procedure of a solemn rite, is difficult to sustain conceptually, and I am unsure how one could fruitfully argue this point towards any rationally and inferentially valid conclusion, simply because we are nowadays unaware of how those ritual forms were enacted.

To add a third aspect to this uncommon composition of character, Vyāsa is one of the *cirañjīvi*, that is, one of those who live forever or until the end of

15 Marcel Proust in his *A La Recherche du Temps Perdu* somewhat approximates to this literary model of conjoint narrative systems.

the present Kali *yuga* and who never perish; thus in that sense he is immortal and non-human and his understanding and knowledge of the *Great Bhārata* is practically and most efficiently undying and shall never decay.[16] What Vyāsa knows therefore is absolute, in creation, in intervention and in discretionary initiation.

It is notable that the *ṛṣi* is absent from the Virāṭa *parvan*. There is only the one scene in this book – the marriage of Arjuna's son at the end of the *parvan* to Uttarā, the daughter of the king – which bears any significance to the overall narrative: for she is to become the mother of Parikṣit, the future king. There is an extremely archaic episode of chariot fighting in which the defeat of the Dhārtarāṣṭras occurs, which is when they raid the Virāṭas in order to steal cattle. This event, however, has little relevance to the plot, apart from being the finest description of chariot warfare in the poem, bringing to the work an impression of genuine and material antiquity.

Similarly, once the Sabhā *parvan* opens, when Kṛṣṇa Vāsudeva has made his entry into the poem, first appearing at the wedding ceremonies of the half-brothers, it is Kṛṣṇa who now begins to take influential precedence with the young Pāṇḍavas, rather than Vyāsa. Thus Vyāsa is not present in the Sabhā *parvan*, except for one brief moment when he enters the poem at V,65,8, during Saṃjaya's embassy to the Hāstinapura court, when he once more suddenly emerges into the narrative, and then at V,67,11 he admonishes Dhṛtarāṣṭra towards a policy of peace-making. On this latter occasion, his words remain unusually feckless and it is as if this is a random editorial inclusion into the epic: this seems to be a line that has been slipped in for the purpose of appearance only, insofar as it possesses no narrative force or consequence.

Why the *ṛṣi* plays no significant role in these two *parvans* is pertinent to one's conception and understanding of the nature of the plot. Does his absence indicate that this part of the poem – 8,746 verses, according to the *parvasaṃgraha* – is actually only story and possesses no bearing upon the fundamental design of the narrative? Certainly, one could make such an assertion concerning the Virāṭa *parvan*, but the Sabhā *parvan* presents scenes that are vital to what we now know as the 'plot' of the *Great Bhārata*. Such scenes relate to the destabilizing *rājasūya* ceremony, the irreversible crisis of gambling and the dreadful abjection of Draupadī; all are instances which are essential and indispensable to the plot as we presently think of the work. Without the occurrence of these events, how would the poem have moved towards the terrible destruction of Kurukṣetra?

16 Paraśurāma is another of these timeless figures who appears in the epic poem; he is the paramount martial *guru* of the work.

It is strange though that during this crucially important fifth *parvan* Vyāsa is so apart from the narrative, and it is as if the degree of dramatic inevitability of these three instances are not able to be influenced by the *ṛṣi*, for without these circumstances there would be no plot. Thus, one might argue that the absence of Vyāsa as a character is a necessary condition during these occasions, that is, if he had been actively present then such disastrous transitions in the plot would not have happened. This is to argue somewhat reductively, however, yet the presence and absence of Vyāsa both have direct consequence on the order of narration, and in this light his *inaction* is just as crucial to the workings of plot as his *action.*

JAYA

Let us now address what happens during the four central Kurukṣetra Books and examine how Vyāsa influences or controls their narration and, also, how he appears as an active character during this part of the poem.

Vyāsa, at the outset of the dreadful battle at Kurukṣetra, presents himself to his son Dhṛtarāṣṭra and predicts what is about to happen. He says,

> VI,2,4: *te haniṣyanti saṃgrāme samāsādyetaretaram*
> Having assembled, they shall kill each other in battle.

Once again the prophetic speech act of the *ṛṣi* soon takes effect, and in the course of 18 days this becomes true. This is bivalent in form, of course, as we have seen elsewhere, for on the one hand Vyāsa is the poet who is said to compose this epic and so he is controlling the narrative, yet on the other hand, as a prophet his words are also efficacious and the speech act is doubly efficient in consequence. It is at this point, as we noted in Chapter 2, that Vyāsa endows Dhṛtarāṣṭra's poet, Saṃjaya, with his divine vision in order that the blind old *rāja* might hear of the combat. Vyāsa reassures the king that the fame of the conflict shall not perish, for he himself will report it. He says,

> VI,2,13: *ahaṃ ca kīrtim eteṣāṃ kurūṇāṃ bharatarṣabha*
> *pāṇḍavānāṃ ca sarveṣāṃ prathayiṣyāmi mā śucaḥ*
> O bull of the Bharatas I shall proclaim the fame
> Of all these Kurus and Pāṇḍavas … Do not grieve.

This statement refers to what Vyāsa shall do in the future, yet it is actually happening in both the past and the present, simultaneously. Such is the compression and density of time with the *Great Bhārata*, where events become so ambiguous, and yet it is this quality of *nuance* that supplies the poem with its conceptual beauty. Also, as we know, fame for a *kṣatriya* is more important than life itself.[17] This verbal *fame* will become the fundamental matter of the *Great Bhārata.*

There now follows a lengthy portrayal of 52 *ślokas* depicting all the ghastly portents and sanguinary omens which precede the battle, and there then occurs that most significant statement which we have already discussed in the previous chapter, *dhyānam anvagamat param*, 'he practiced high meditation' (VI,4,1).

Vyāsa blames Duryodhana, his own grandson, at this point, again speaking as a character in the poem rather than its poetic creator, for he says, *kālo'yaṃ putrarūpeṇa tava jāto*, 'This death has been born with the form of your son' (VI,4,5). It is remarkable how the poet-originators of Epic *Mahābhārata* are able to move among these various aspects and dimensions of the character Vyāsa in this manner: he is *the* poet of the work, its prophet within the poem, and also, like Bhīṣma, a momentously authoritative character when moral discrimination is required.

It is telling, therefore, that during the Chariot Song of Vāsudeva, Kṛṣṇa tells Arjuna, *munīnām apy ahaṃ vyāsaḥ*, 'so among the renouncers I am Vyāsa' (VI,32,37). During this pluralistic and monotheistic chant in which Kṛṣṇa proclaims his unity and identity with all cosmic forces, he now also assumes into himself this creative presence of the *ṛṣi*. At the end of the Gītā's proclamation, Saṃjaya, who has performed this song, says,

> VI,40,75: *vyāsaprasādāc śrutavān etad guhyam ahaṃ param*
> *yogaṃ yogeṣvarāt kṛṣṇāt sākṣāt kathayataḥ svayam*
> I heard that ultimate yogic mystery because of the grace of Vyāsa,
> From Kṛṣṇa's telling, the lord of *yoga* in person.

According to this poet, then, it was the mercurial virtuosity of Vyāsa himself that supplied the actual practical medium for the expression of Kṛṣṇa's Gītā, a statement which fits with our fundamental understanding of the poem – especially in its form of *Jaya* – as having come from the poetic and exuberant genius of the progenitor of the epic himself. This is a remarkable claim and is a message that is often overlooked.

Similarly, when Bhīṣma sings a long hymn in praise of Kṛṣṇa Vāsudeva, given in the voice of Brahma in person, he says that he heard all this from

17 In McGrath, 2004a, I studied this ancient warrior disposition towards fame, particularly as it applied to Karṇa, a hero who, like Homeric Achilles, is prepossessed by his potential relationship with this idea and its future substance. Such a passion is in fact transcendental in consequence.

Vyāsa (VI,62,27). Thus characters in the poem, when performing in a devotional or inspired fashion – concerning the divine Kṛṣṇa – always revert to the mediating superiority of Vyāsa, in terms of his knowledge and its expression, of the sharing of such sublime intelligence, and of that unspeakable visionary capacity which he both mortally and immortally embodies.

Likewise, Bhīṣma, as he lies morbid upon a couch of arrows, when the hero Karṇa approaches him in order to receive benediction, tells the warrior that he had heard from Vyāsa about how Karṇa was not in fact the son of Radhā but that he was born of Kuntī (VI,117,7). Again, the audience perceives how the omniscient *ṛṣi* is constantly overseeing the narrative, informing it, participating in it and always moderating its evolution in ways that are often profoundly discreet, undisclosed, and which are present and effective often only by *intimation* or hearsay.

In the great Droṇa *parvan* Vyāsa scarcely appears except at the end, where he sings a hymn of praise to Nārāyaṇa – or Kṛṣṇa Vāsudeva in his divinized being – who is said to be *putro dharmasya*, 'the son of Dharma', which is unusual, for this is typically the patronym of *rāja* Yudhiṣṭhira (VII,172,51). Vyāsa also says that this figure is *pūrvaṣām api pūrvajaḥ*, 'hence the eldest born of the oldest', who after terrific austerities receives a vision of Rudra.

In the voice of Nārāyaṇa-Kṛṣṇa, Vyāsa then sings a long praise song to Rudra, which is virtually monotheistic, and within this Vyāsa actually impersonates the deity – here named Nīlakaṇṭha – offering a favour to Nārāyaṇa (VII,172,74–90). So the sequence of known voices here, in terms of poetry, is: Ugraśravas > (Vaiśaṃpāyana) > Saṃjaya > Vyāsa > Nārāyaṇa > Rudra, although it is Vyāsa who is supposed to have originated the first poem and to be also actually speaking in this instance. Such is the polyvalent and circular imbrication of voice and drama which the poets and editors have caused to be inherent to the *Great Bhārata*. As we observed before, this is literally unreasonable and yet it supplies the poem with its beautiful and immaculate complexity, for there is this coruscation of so many simultaneous or coincidental narrative dimensions.

Incidentally, such praise hymns for Kṛṣṇa or Rudra-Śiva usually occur at the end of *parvans* due to the ease with which such songs could be appended by editors to the main body of the poem. This is a phenomenon or a sign of literacy, for during preliterate times these additions could be made anywhere in the text with facility.

Towards the beginning of the Śalya *parvan* when Satyaki and Dhṛṣṭadyumna capture Saṃjaya – the poet who is performing this chapter and who also, like Vyāsa, appears here as a character in the poem – they are about to kill the poet. Vyāsa appears and orders them to desist. Thus it is as if the envelope of poetry is being reversed and the speaker becomes a figure in the epic who is suddenly being *spoken*, which is again paradoxical. It is due to incongruous moments like this that the poem – I would argue – becomes a seamless and irreducible work of art; yet it is faultless, for the usual mode of narrative causality is made acceptably illogical. Vyāsa says,

> IX,28,37: *muchyatāṃ saṃjayo jīvan na hantavyaḥ kathaṃcana*
> Release Saṃjaya! Living, he is in no way to be killed!

Later in the epics, in a similar instant of prohibition Vyāsa speaks in the dual with Nārada, a rare moment in the poem where two voices are delivered simultaneously: *ṛṣī ucatuḥ*, says the direction, 'both *ṛṣis* spoke'. They say,

> X,14,16: *nānāśastravidaḥ pūrve ye'py atītā mahārathāḥ*
> *naitad astraṃ manuṣyeṣu taiḥ prayuktaṃ kathaṃcana*
> The deceased great charioteers who possessed the knowledge of various missiles in the past –
> That missile was never discharged by them amongst humanity.

The situation occurs at the end of the Sauptika *parvan* where Aśvatthāman and Arjuna have released terrible projectiles against each other, weapons that would have dreadful consequences for all of life: hence the two *ṛṣis* interpose themselves to prevent such weaponry from having effect, pacifying the energy of the armament, *lokānāṃ hitakāmyayā*, 'with desire for the good of the worlds'.[18]

Arjuna, observing the immediate presence of Vyāsa and Nārada, withdraws his weapon, but Aśvatthāman cannot do this and simply redirects the course of his missile. Vyāsa urges the latter warrior to retract his discharge, promising that *rāja* Yudhiṣṭhira will pardon him for all the horrors of the previous night, when the sons of Draupadī and others were assassinated during darkness. In return, he tells Aśvatthāman that he must relinquish a jewel which the young hero wears on his forehead for the purpose of protection. Aśvatthāman agrees to the exchange, although he is unable to call back the missile and is only

---

18 In the *mahābhāratasravaṇamahimā*, the final *adhyāya* of the Bombay Edition, the *parvans* are listed, yet there is no mention of the Sauptika *parvan* in this sequencing, implying that it was once not part of the poem's plot. Curiously, during this last chapter of the poem there are several references to *pustaka*, 'book', which give a late date to this part of the epic (XVIII,5,73 and 77, BE).

competent to redirect its force; this he does, sending destruction towards the wombs of the Pāṇḍava wives.

Vyāsa simply asserts this change, saying, *evaṃ kuru*, 'do this', as if his speech act will charge the redirection with its efficacy (X,15,32). It is Kṛṣṇa Vāsudeva, however, who promises to revive the destroyed foetus of Abhimanyu's widow, Uttarā, stating that this infant, *kururāja bhaviṣyati*, 'he shall become the king of Kurus' (X,16,15). It is notable that the poets allow this transition of the authority and power of Vyāsa – as director of the narration – to be passed towards heroic Kṛṣṇa at this point and that it is *not* Vyāsa who performs the revival; this is not a kind of action or event which the audience has heard of before now, as the master of the plot's advance is no longer the old *ṛṣi* but has become the young Yādava hero and peer of Yudhiṣṭhira.

During the early *adhyāyas* of the Strī *parvan*, when ancient Dhṛtarāṣṭra is overwhelmed with grief and disquiet for the death of all but one of his male offspring, Vyāsa is there, along with Vidura and Saṃjaya, consoling the old man's tears. Vyāsa tells his son, the blind king, how once he had been assumed into the heaven or the *sabhā* of Indra and how there he looked down upon the mortal world: *tatra cāpi mayā dṛṣṭvā pṛthivī*, 'and so there the earth was witnessed by me' (XI,8,21). The earth then spoke with Viṣṇu, says Vyāsa, forecasting how the Dhārtarāṣṭras would all be annihilated in the coming war at Kurukṣetra. This is an unusual scene, for it is the only time that the *ṛṣi* moves into a supernatural location and participates in unearthly discourse. Arjuna and Nārada often behave in such a manner, but this has not occurred in the life cycle of Vyāsa, who appears to have been able to travel to this cosmic place at will. Having described the total destruction caused by the battle and how this was unavoidable, he tells the old *rāja* that

XI,8,34: *etat te sarvam ākhyātaṃ devaguhyaṃ sanātanam*
All that divine eternal secret has been described to you.

This is also one of the few occasions where Vyāsa ascribes to the events of the poem an ulterior and supernal state of causality; others often speak in such a fashion, citing *daivam*, 'destiny', but it is rare for the *ṛṣi* to admit to such efficacy, for it necessarily diminishes his personal degree of influence in the poem's creation, development and prophetic narration.

He is soon to address his daughter-in-law, the wife of Dhṛtarāṣṭra, in a similar mode; in her case it is not the emotion of grief which needs to be appeased and mollified but the anger and rage which she feels for the Pāṇḍava half-brothers who have killed all but one of her many sons. On this occasion,

Vyāsa is keen to prevent Gāndhārī from cursing Yudhiṣṭhira, knowing how potent and successful her punitive wrath would be, and he admonishes her to be forgiving rather than vindictive.

XI,13,5: *divyena cakṣuṣā paśyan manasān uddhatena ca*
sarvaprāṇabhṛitāṃ bhāvaṃ sa tatra samabudhyata
Seeing humanity by divinely aroused vision,
He there perceived the being of all bearers of life.

It is with this comprehension of the cosmic quality of life that the *ṛṣi* simply appears when his direction of the narrative is required, and his words of compassion soothe the rage of Gāndhārī; he is verbally and practically able to combine the supernal with the worldly. He tells her,

XI,13,7: *na kopaḥ pāṇḍave kāryo gāndhāri śamam āpnuhi*
O Gāndhārī, seize upon peace, do not make anger against the Pāṇḍava!

In the ensuing scene, it is said of her that *apaśyat tatra [...] sarvaṃ divyena cakṣuṣā*, 'she there saw everything with divine vision', a capacity which – like Saṃjaya – she has received from the *ṛṣi* (XI,16,1).[19] Gāndhārī then proceeds about the field, indicating, describing and singing lamentably for all her deceased male kin. Let us recall that on her marriage with the blind Dhṛtarāṣṭra this bride covered her eyes forever with a cloth so that she would be equal to him in visual deprivation.

Just as Saṃjaya with his divine vision became the substitute for Vyāsa when the great battle commenced, so, now, once the fallen warriors are to be lamented it is the visionary old queen – as his verbal proxy – who takes on this role of public and formal mourning, in a manner that is thoroughly deictic and evocative. Both she and Saṃjaya make use of the identical imperative and indicative voice with the word *paśya*, 'look!'[20]

19 Arguably, this divine vision is ultimately endowed upon the audience of the poem, who perceive *everything* that is happening in the narrative which has been visualized by the poets. Such an endowment is the accomplishment of the *Great Bhārata*, causing it to become *the* classic song of India.

20 The word *paśya* is part of the charioteer's lexicon, used when he draws the attention of his hero to a scene or individual on the battlefield. In McGrath, 2011, pp. 17–18, I show how Gāndhārī employs this manner of speech.

ŚĀNTI

The poet Vyāsa now enters upon a different kind of bearing and speech as the epic poem engages with a new form of poetry, one that has little dramatic and literal connection with what preceded it during the previous 11 *parvans*. I have argued elsewhere that this second half of the epic is a work principally of edition rather than of direct inspiration.[21]

The *parvan* opens with a long scene depicting the anxiety and sorrow of *rāja* Yudhiṣṭhira.[22] Vyāsa is present and speaks to convince the king to rule with dignity and vigour and to abjure grief. Let us remember, however, that it was Yudhiṣṭhira's claim to paramount kingship at Hāstinapura – through the performance of the wrecked *rājasūya* ritual – which caused the war and the almost complete destruction of the *kṣatriya* community in that kingdom; there is no doubt as to his personal culpability here. Vyāsa, after telling many illuminating stories about how other kings had behaved in the past, says,

> XII,25,7: *sarvamedhāśvamedhābhyāṃ yajasva kurunandana*
> O joy of the Kurus sacrifice with the Horse Sacrifice and the All-Sacrifice.

Vyāsa and others continue to speak to the king for a dozen *adhyāyas*, attempting to convince him about how appropriate his new authority is. After this, Vyāsa instructs the king to go to Kurukṣetra, where the recumbent and morbid Bhīṣma, the ancient of the clan, will advise him further about his new political and sovereign role. Thus is *rāja* Yudhiṣṭhira directed towards what will become the teaching of the Śānti *parvan* and then towards the practice of an *āśvamedha*. Once again the audience perceives the *ṛṣi* as one who directs the movement of characters and narrative.

It would appear that Vyāsa is present for the long discourse of the Śānti *parvan*, for it is said that, when the Pāṇḍavas and Yādavas arrive at Kurukṣetra,

> XII,59,3: *vyāsādīn abhivādya ṛṣīn sarvais taiś cābhinanditāḥ*
> *niṣedur abhito bhīṣmaṃ parivārya samantataḥ*
> Having greeted Vyāsa and other *ṛṣis* and applauded by all those,
> They sat down in the round having encircled Bhīṣma.

21 McGrath, 2018b.

22 Yudhiṣṭhira summarizes his guilt most extensively as he himself perceives this at XII,27,3–25; he concludes by declaring his intention to relinquish life.

His presence becomes blurred, however, as the vast oration continues, and at the 224th *adhyāya* Bhīṣma is quoting from a long discourse which Vyāsa is said to have delivered to his son Śuka (XII,224,11 to 246,15).[23] It is as if Vyāsa is not present during this time, such is the quality of the reported speech; I would argue that this is due to the nature of how the narratives of the 12th and 13th *parvans* have been composed, made up in an editorial manner of learned discourse and select treatise.

Yet in a contrary fashion, let us again recall, however, that it is Vaiśaṃpāyana who is actually speaking and who is reciting what he had learned when Vyāsa first delivered the *Bhārata*. At this point the practical or lexical distinction between *Bhārata* and *Great Bhārata* is subject to a most thorough ellipsis.

Once the plot – the narrative which presently circulates about *rāja* Yudhiṣṭhira – re-engages at the outset of the Āśvamedhika *parvan*, Vyāsa returns to the poem and addresses the king, questioning his excessive grief and remorse, reiterating what Kṛṣṇa says, *tyaja śokaṃ*, 'abandon sorrow' (XIV,2,8). This occurs after the obsequies for old Bhīṣma have just been completed. As we noted earlier, Bhīṣma is the only truly significant peer of Vyāsa in the poem, the former being born of the Gaṅgā and the latter being born of the Yamunā; Bhīṣma is thoroughly mortal, however.

Yudhiṣṭhira then requests of Kṛṣṇa – who has consistently acted as his royal and kingly equal – that he be permitted to renounce kingship and seek a renunciant life in the wilderness, for he wishes, *gantuṃ tapovanam*, 'to go to the forest of withdrawal' (XIV,2,12). Then Vyāsa intervenes, saying to the king, *bālyena muhyase*, 'you are deluded by naiveté', and he advises Yudhiṣṭhira to perform high rituals.

XIV,3,8: *rājasūyāśvamedhau ca sarvamedhaṃ ca bhārata*
naramedhaṃ ca nṛpate tvam āhara yudhiṣṭhira
O Bhārata, offer both the *rājasūya* and a horse sacrifice and
The universal sacrifice and human sacrifice, O you king,
Yudhiṣṭhira!

---

23 The generation and birth of this son Śuka is given in XII,311, where Vyāsa uncontrollably ejaculates his semen: he had been attempting to ignite a fire with *araṇī*, 'two kindling sticks', and had been attracted to an *apsarā*, who then changed her form into that of a parrot or *śukī*. The son who was spontaneously generated at this instant became known as Śuka. The story of Śuka exists outside the narrative of the *Mahābhārata* proper, and it has neither influence on nor presence in the poem's plot apart from itself; it is completely part of the story and is an edifying micronarrative. When Śuka finally achieves spiritual liberation and vanishes into the utmost cosmos, Vyāsa experiences terrific grief; but then the Mahādeva appears and assures him that his blessed son will always be at his side in the form of a *chāya*, 'shadowy figure' (XII,320,37). At this, Vyāsa is gratified.

The wealth required to accomplish such ceremonies is huge, and so Vyāsa then proceeds to relate a lengthy story about the mythical *rāja* Marutta and how he acquired quantities of gold by visiting the Himālaya (XIV,4,2–10,36). Then, just as with the Gītā, the Chariot Song of Kṛṣṇa that preceded the fighting at Kurukṣetra, so now the narrative of the Anugītā is delivered, and this precedes the combat which Arjuna is about to enter as he follows the sacrificial horse about Bhāratavarṣa and protects it from assailants.[24] As we have already observed, even though the two later *parvans* – 12 and 13 – are delivered by Vaiśaṃpāyana, they are not in the substantive or formal style of the earlier books and are as if remote from the world view of Vyāsa as we have seen and inferred from those previous parts of the poem. The Anugītā is of a likeness here in that it stands fully apart from the plot of the poem, and even considered as story it is distant and removed from the overall work; it does not relate in any way with the world of Vyāsa as we presently comprehend it.

Once this wealth has been acquired, Vyāsa then charges the king to commence the ritual, saying, *yajasva vājimedhena vidhivad*, 'sacrifice appropriately with the horse sacrifice' (XIV,70,15). He then gives more specific directions as to how this is to be performed and by whom (XVI,71,3–6 and 14–21).[25] Months later, when the prolonged peregrinations of the animal are complete, the actual rites occur and the horse is immolated; Vyāsa and his disciples formally praise the king, and then *rāja* Yudhiṣṭhira correctly offers gifts to the *brāhmaṇas* and to Vyāsa himself: *prādāt [...] vyāsāya tu vasuṃdharām*, 'he gave to Vyāsa the earth' (XIV,91,7). This is of course returned with equal formality, thus establishing that primary and thoroughly reciprocal old-time relationship between king and *maharṣi* or *brāhmaṇa.*

In the next *parvan*, once again the audience hears of how Vyāsa suddenly appears and continues to sustain the plot in that he directs the king to allow aged Dhṛtarāṣṭra to retire towards the forest along with a small retinue. Yudhiṣṭhira naturally accords with this directive, saying that Vyāsa is his father, king and *guru* (XV,8,8). Vyāsa then magically vanishes.

Then, at a later occasion, when Gāndhārī expresses her inordinate grief to Vyāsa for the loss of her 99 sons, the *ṛṣi* promises to produce a vision for her of all these deceased, saying, *drakṣyasi gāndhāri putrān bhrātṝn*, 'Gāndhārī, you shall witness the sons [and] brothers' (XV,39,1). He then arranges that all the deceased *kṣatriyas* from the fighting at Kurukṣetra arise for a few moments out of the Gaṅgā. The poets say,

24 For an analysis of these events, see McGrath, 2016, ch. 4.

25 In McGrath, 2017a, ch. 2,v,3, I examine how *rāja* Yudhiṣṭhira accomplishes this rite.

XV,40,21: *dhṛtarāṣṭras tu tān sarvān paśyan divyena cakṣuṣā*
mumude bharataśreṣṭha prasādāt tasya vai muneḥ
Then Dhṛtarāṣṭra seeing all those by divine vision,
O best of the Bharatas, he was joyous, due to the grace of that *muni* [Vyāsa].

It is notable that the dead are here said to inhabit the sacred river; they are not in an underworld situation nor are they anywhere that is *upward* or superterrestrial. The location of the deceased psyches of the dead is never firmly indicated in the epic and is frequently various, and it is as if many traditions are blurred in an attempt at synopsis.

Being congenitally blind, Dhṛtarāṣṭra had never actually visually perceived his sons or any of his kin before that instant, so this magical occasion was doubly satisfying for him. Once again, as with Saṃjaya, Yudhiṣṭhira and Gāndhārī, it is Vyāsa who supplies these witnesses with divine vision. Just as Vyāsa is said to be the first to visualize – in words – the *Bhārata* poem for the audience, it is Vyāsa the *magus* who is able to bring superhuman perception to the characters so that they might visually participate in the usually unseen inner workings of the poem. All this, of course, being visualized in words is therefore 'seen' by the audience, for the acoustic signal materially and mysteriously translates into visual signs, in a cognitive sense. This *audience* has existed for more than two and a half thousand years, although nowadays it is the art of cinema and television which primarily functions as the medium of eidetic communication.

The poets then do something that is textually insufficient, for the speaker suddenly moves from being Vaiśaṃpāyana to Ugraśravas. *Rāja* Janamejaya had unexpectedly interrupted and commented on this joy of Dhṛtarāṣṭra – which was occurring five generations previously – and requests that now Vaiśaṃpāyana grant him a similar vision, for he wished to see his own father, Parikṣit, the grandson of Arjuna, in a similar luminary fashion. Vaiśaṃpāyana of course has no mystical capacity to grant this, but Ugraśravas, who is addressing the *brāhmaṇas* in the Naimiṣa forest – as reported by an unnamed master poet – says that, *vyāsaḥ […] prasādam akarod dhīmān ānāyac ca parikṣitam*, 'Vyāsa performed a mediation and brought Parikṣit' (XV,43,6).

Janamejaya thus sees the psyche of his expired father, and moreover, he ritually bathes the ancestor: *mudito janamejayaḥ / pitaraṃ snāpayāmāsa svayaṃ*, 'the happy Janamejaya himself ritually bathed the father' (XV,43,9). Such a brief and dexterous narrative sequence is remarkable and, to my knowledge, unique; for Vyāsa the proto-poet is not only appearing as a character in the poem but he is here also appearing on the occasion of the much later performance of that poem itself. Thus three dimensions of time are simultaneously being activated and concentrated in his single person.

This is one of the most supra-dimensional instants in the *Great Bhārata* and tells us, as analysts, something about how those early Bronze Age poets thought and how they worked with the various temporal frames of the song, not as a mnemonic system but as a unified narrative order. Presumably, for them there was nothing irrational or dramatically inconsistent with this scene and the unities of time can be easily substituted like this without calling into question the nature of temporal logic. This is simply an aspect of their great artistry and also of their profound supernal comprehension of the universe; the necessity of strict temporal sequence in that culture was not as autarchic as it is for us moderns.

At the end of the *Great Bhārata*, the poets say of the epic that it was, *kṛṣṇena muninā [...] niyataṃ satyavādinā*, 'composed by the truth-telling ascetic Kṛṣṇa' (XVIII,5,31). As we have seen, this has been composed with so much anterior poetic tradition already in mind, and yet specifically composed with the artifice of a discrete poetic event. It has also been composed with Vyāsa as a speaker of great and forceful dramatic character, one who accomplishes much in the plot simply by virtue of his speech acts. Finally, it has been composed with such complex narration as a metaphor of human consciousness itself: for the human mind is polyvalent and multifarious, and it is not at all a unified system of awareness for it does not possess temporal unity. One should neither omit nor ignore the distinction here – in compositional attitudes and techniques – between poets and editors.

The point being that there are many concurrent and simultaneous kinds of historical sequence or series of events that exist in the human psyche, and these run concomitantly without any appearance or experience of the irrationally ambiguous. In that view the *Great Bhārata* narrative itself is inherently metaphorical, manifesting the multitudinous dimensionality of human consciousness and cognition. *Homo narrans* is able to accomplish this kind of poetry, something which in the material world of annual and linear days and nights is impossible but not inconceivable.

Towards the end of the poem, when Arjuna has lost his friend and charioteer Kṛṣṇa and becomes not only overcome by grief but also physically and martially weakened by the absence of his heroic and charioteering companion, he goes to the *āśram* of Vyāsa.[26] The audience never hears anything about the geographical location of this site. Arjuna speaks of his sorrow to Vyāsa and claims that he no longer wishes to live without the company of Kṛṣṇa, his friend:

---

26 In McGrath, 2016, ch. 4, I study these events that occur towards the end of Arjuna's life.

XVI,9,23: *vinā janārdanaṃ vīraṃ nāhaṃ jīvitum utsahe*
Without the warrior Janārdana I am not able to live.

Vyāsa consoles him and then tells him that his, Arjuna's, life is soon to end. Once more, the audience observe not only how the *maharṣi* dominates the plot, actively, practically or simply in terms of foresight, but also how he influences the affective being of other characters.

From the point of view of Vyāsa as the creator of the poem, this kind of dramatic poetry also includes instants where the emotions of the heroic persons are discreetly portrayed by the poets, something which is in excess of what it is that is occurring explicitly in the language of the characters. This would be to display the ironic anger of Draupadī, for instance, at III,13,43–116, when she berates Kṛṣṇa Vāsudeva, or when she and Yudhiṣṭhira are arguing in the forest (III,28–33), or the many occasions where grief is being displayed. Characters – and therefore audience – are able to apprehend the undisclosed affective world of other characters, perceiving what is active in their *minds*. Again, it is the play of narrative *qua* metaphor that is at work, for the communication is not overtly explicit on such occasions.

In such moments the audience or the reader becomes aware of how the speakers in the poem are actually *feeling* as they converse with other speakers. Such emotions are not made obvious but are there to be recognized via the poetic use of words. Narrative is able to indicate this aspect of human discourse without being objectively candid about what is happening within the affective psyche of a character, supplying shadow, as it were, to the delineation which language can achieve. Thus the heroes and heroines within the poem are not merely perceived as two-dimensional figures but are also known to possess a psychic or mental interiority – a further and insightful dimension of consciousness – particularly as it concerns emotion and dubiety. This implication is received by the attentive audience or the aware close reader and is the work of a literary connoisseur.

Hence the truth of this fiction which derives from the mentality and person of *ṛṣi* Vyāsa is delivered in what is virtually a tripartite fashion: human, superhuman and supernatural. This is what makes the *Mahābhārata* such a unique and wonderful poem of consummate artistry, and to my present knowledge there is nothing like it, in terms of such sophisticated supercomplexity, poetic architecture and such implied yet verbally undisclosed insight. At the end of this book we shall turn to another epic song which approximates this literary or poetic situation – but differently – and see how we might further comprehend the art of Vyāsa, but from a comparative perspective.

Chapter 5

AFTER VYĀSA

VYĀSA, as a poet, is often superseded in the poem by other voices. We have just discussed the last seven books of the epic, where he was simply a nominal presence; let us now closely read some of the passages that occur at the outset of the work in the complicated Ādi *parvan*, where the poetry of Vyāsa is logically absent and the poem is more the work of editorial practice as the poets talk *about* Vyāsa and his life. This chapter returns to and advances a point initially raised earlier, in Chapter 2.

In the full and complete poem, there are three discourses between interlocutors that constitute the poem's narrative: there is that of Śaunaka and Ugraśravas, then later there is that of Vaiśaṃpāyana and Janamejaya, and then, within that cycle there is the core poetry which is exchanged between Saṃjaya and old Dhṛtarāṣṭra. These are the three dramatic dialogues which bear the transport of the poem, the second being the most weighty and substantive.

These are the three frames of the epic, as it were, all of which are here represented in the Ādi *parvan* and spoken by the anonymous proto-poet whom we cannot ever identify. All three of these modes are present in some indicated form during this preliminary chapter as the overall narrative is slowly and incrementally previsited. What I would like to demonstrate now is the strange refraction of summaries which happens at the commencement of the poem, in which the master narrative is exposed in various abridgements and extractions which are frequently not concordant.

As we have seen, it is the *sūta* Ugraśravas who commences the *Great Bhārata* as we have it now in the Pune Critical Edition (PCE). The first time that the audience hear about what Ugraśravas intends to tell the *brahmarṣis* whom he has encountered in the Naimiṣa forest, he introduces the promised epic with a brief cosmogony, beginning at I,1,20. Following this is a cursory description of Vyāsa, 'the son of Satyavatī', and his many great vocations. The *Bhārata* poem – in *précis* form – does not begin to open until the 65th *śloka*, where the first words are *duryodhano manyumayo*, 'Duryodhana made of wrath', and then the poet engages with the first metaphor of the poem, that of a tree.[1] He says that the Pāṇḍavas and the Dhārtarāṣṭras are each a *mahādrumaḥ*, 'great tree'.

A quick summary depiction of a possible Bhārata continues, in which Ugraśravas, for 29 *ślokas*, relates some of the juvenile experiences of the Pāṇḍavas and quickly rehearses a few of the focal points of the poem's plot. He then imitates the speech of Dhṛtarāṣṭra for almost a hundred verses as the old *rāja* summarizes the plot from a retrospective point of view. This is the only time in the *Great Bhārata* that this mournful monologue of the aged king is heard.

Ugraśravas, during this *introit*, imitates the poet Saṃjaya speaking with Dhṛtarāṣṭra, which is another irrational instance, for the old *rāja* is expressing his terrific grief at how so much had been lost – that is, he is explicitly grieving *post hoc*, after the defeat of Kurukṣetra and during the lament he recapitulates the complete Bhārata plot, couched in the emotive language of sorrow (I,1,102–58). This is not so much a narrative as a series of paratactically connected exclamations. The speech is 'after the event' and, paradoxically, all that it states has not yet occurred, for the Bhārata has not yet begun to be declaimed: it is absolutely proleptic, or what in cinema studies is referred to as *fast-forwarding*.

Thus far, two separate and divergent summations of the plot have occurred along with a few elements of minor story that is preceded by a succinct cosmogony.

The personal voice of Ugraśravas re-engages at I,1,19, where he ceases to sing of the house of Hāstinapura in the enacted or performed speech of Dhṛtarāṣṭra and Saṃjaya, as he reverts to speaking about Vyāsa and how that poet initially created and proclaimed the work. Ugraśravas continues to respond to the questions of the Naimiṣa renunciants and then reviews the contents of the epic in a twofold fashion: this is the *anukramaṇī*, the 'catalogue' of 100 micronarratives, and the *parvasaṃgraha*, the 'summaries' of the 18 *parvans*.

These constitute two further summations of the poem, and here story is included with plot.

The *parvan* continues with the poet describing events that are not yet in fact part of the Bhārata: the third *adhyāya* is devoted to a rite which *rāja* Janamejaya performed at Kurukṣetra, which is of course taking place long *after* the plot of the epic had closed. This is not even *story* as the events here concern a period that comes after the plot of the *Great Bhārata*, and much of this is in prose, not verse. These passages are what I would assert are the work of editorial

1 Heroes as trees, mountains, fires and sometimes rivers deliver key metaphors and similes in the epic.

addition, for what they do is supply a background to the conversation which led to Janamejaya's conquering of Takṣaśilā and his subsequent snake sacrifice there: which is where the *Bhārata* was initially composed and declaimed by *ṛṣi* Vyāsa, but that too was much later in time.

Then, with the outset of the fourth *adhyāya*, the poem as we have it now recommences with the anonymous master poet declaiming that Ugraśravas had once more arrived at the Naimiṣa forest where Śaunaka and his ascetic band were gathered. It is as if the poem is renewing itself and beginning once again, virtually in the same form and reiterating the origins and aetiology of the work. Commissioned to sing of the Bhārgava lineage, Ugraśravas confesses that he learned this from his father, who had received the words from Vaiśaṃpāyana (I,5,4–5). Ugraśravas repeats this claim later, saying that this knowledge was received by his father from Vyāsa, and he says of this song that it was, *kṛṣṇadvaipāyanaproktaṃ naimiṣāranyavāsinaḥ*, 'declaimed by Kṛṣṇa Dvaipāyana to the dwellers in the Naimiṣa Forest' (I,13,6). These lines contain references to divine agents like Garuḍa and Nārāyaṇa, who are not ancient deities but divinities drawn from the centuries of inchoate Hinduism at the beginning of the first millennium CE.

This is certainly *not* the Bhārata but something else; it is not material that concerns the plot of the epic, yet, as we argued in Chapter 2, what came to be Sukthankar's hypothetical *Bhārgava Recension* is now substantiated with all this material that tells of the emergent clan of eponymous Bhṛgu. As we know, this has certainly nothing to do with Vyāsa's *Bhārata*.

The discourse of Ugraśravas continues in past form, telling of the ancestral world of the clan and family until this converges with the Bhārata at the 48th *adhyāya* when the poet speaks of the snake sacrifice of Janamejaya, mentioning that Vyāsa held the office of *sadasya* at this rite (I,47,7). Curiously, there is no indication of there being any performance of the Bhārata during this ceremony and it is as if an ellipsis has occurred; elsewhere in the poem it is always declared that this was the first instancing of the epic. Only in a later chapter does the audience hear of the epic's first occasioning:

> I,53,31: *karmāntareṣvakathayan dvijā vedāśrayāḥ kathāḥ*
> *vyāsas tvakathayan nityam ākhyānāṃ bhāratam mahat*
> The twice-born practitioners of the Vedas proclaimed
> during the spaces in the rite – epics,
> But Vyāsa pronounced the perpetual tale, the vast Bhārata.[2]

2 The terms *ākhyāna*, 'legends', and *kathā* are employed synonymously during these passages.

Ugraśravas, at last commissioned by Bhārgava Śaunaka, says, *kathayiṣyāmi [...] mahābhāratam*, 'I shall declaim the Great Bhārata', and he declares that this will be *manoharṣo*, 'delightful' for him (I,53,35).

Finally, with the 54th *adhyāya*, Ugraśravas at last begins to approach the onset of the song, beginning with what is in effect a hymn to Vyāsa which recapitulates his life, efforts and accomplishments. He refers to Satyavatī here by only using the rare epithet Kālī, telling of how she gave birth to her child (I,54,2). Ugraśravas rehearses the life of Vyāsa in a few lines, speaking about his primary knowledge of the Vedas, his fathering of the two famed sons and his meeting with Janamejaya, who is his great-grandson. It is then that Vyāsa commissions Vaiśaṃpāyana to perform the poem as his deputy, and the word that he uses to designate this song is *bheda*, 'partition', as it occurred between the Pāṇḍavas and Dhārtarāṣṭras (I,54,21–22); the *Bhārata* is to be a poem about this 'separation' or 'division', that is its signifying theme. *Bheda* is hence the master signifier of the plot.

The poem now truly begins – as the second frame, that of Vaiśaṃpāyana –with this poet appropriately proclaiming the greatness and magnificence of Vyāsa, his teacher (I,55,1). He says that he will tell of *bheda* which was caused by the gambling, of the long forest retreat of the Pāṇḍavas and of the battle: these are the three dramatic moments or themes by which he depicts the poem. He actually commences, though, by singing about the youthful rivalries between the two sets of cousins, what in fact is background material (I,55,6).

This retrojective instant speaks of how the young half-brothers had lived in the forest since their father Pāṇḍu expired, and continues from where Ugraśravas had initially and lightly told of their return from the wilderness to Hāstinapura when he had summarized that original time earlier in the poem (I,1,70).

Vaiśaṃpāyana continues his account by speaking of the incipient contention which existed between the Pāṇḍava and Dhārtarāṣṭra adolescents, many of which events are deadly and homicidal and designed to destroy the sons of Kuntī. He tells of how the five half-brothers married Draupadī and then returned to a life in the backwoods, of how Kṛṣṇa Vāsudeva entered the plot and Arjuna also married Kṛṣṇa's sister and of how, during this period, the predatory Arjuna was slowly acquiring supernatural weaponry. He ends with the dice match, although, curiously, he omits the hubristic *rājasūya* ceremony that preceded this and which many have alleged was the true and primary source of *bheda*. Here it is the rigged gambling and the abjection of Draupadī which supplies the necessary condition for imminent warfare. Vaiśaṃpāyana closes his exposition of the *Bhārata* narrative by telling of Duryodhana's demise.[3] This summation continues for 39 *ślokas*, and this is the fifth summary which the audience hear (I,55,4–43).

Thus, before the poem actually commences there are these many outlines which are being delivered, all different and all given in alternate voices and offering varying perspectives on both the plot and story of the epic. It is as if there is much editorial bricolage happening here, as several often non-synoptic condensations of the work are conveyed in a fashion that eschews right concordance. The poem is thus being presented – if not refracted – at its outset and in summary form through many different eyes and voices, supplying numerous dimensions to these preliminary overviews of the narrative; these will all eventually converge in the words of Vaiśṃpāyana, who tells of what he *remembers* Vyāsa as once saying.

So what does it mean to have these two or in fact three opening expositions of the poem, and why have the editors done this? Three poets are engaged here, Ugraśravas, Saṃjaya and Vaiśaṃpāyana, in that order, with Ugraśravas presenting Saṃjaya rather than Vaiśaṃpāyana. This arrangement or these cursory constitutions of the poem are definitely *after* Vyāsa, that is, if what we argued in Chapter 2 is correct: for they relate to the nature of edition rather than that of direct inspiration.

It is as if the Vaiśaṃpāyana opening has had this Ugraśravas performance of 54 *adhyāyas* prefixed to it and the editors have only slightly modified the text so that there is some narrative unity, but this is imperfect and moderately illogical due to Saṃjaya's presence, for he has not even entered the narrative yet. There is therefore much perplexing inconcinnity in this part of the PCE document in terms of how the varying narratives that are associated with Vyāsa tend to compete with each other for precedence, and it is as if the one primary narrative has been refracted into many aspects, proportions and factors.

When urged a second time by *rāja* Janamejaya, Vaiśaṃpāyana now says that his song contains a hundred thousand verses and he then details the spiritual merit that derives from listening to the performance of the epic (I,56,14). As we know, the audience never hear of that hypothetical *Bhārata* which Vyāsa was the first to proclaim. Vaiśaṃpāyana then begins the *Mahābhārata* by telling of *rāja* Vasu, who later acquired the epithet of Uparicara, 'the one who goes above', due to his sky-going ability, a gift from Indra. It was from the semen of Vasu or Uparicara that Satyavatī was born, after gestating in the body of a fish (I,57,50).

3 As we observed above, referring to I,1,65, the first opening of the poem starts with the name of the audacious Duryodhana, and it is extremely pertinent that here, Vaiśaṃpāyana closes his summation with the death of that hero and king.

Thus the poem recommences once again, and Vaiśaṃpāyana opens this song with a hymn that speaks of the making of Vyāsa's mother and how it was that this unique *guru* was generated (I,57,71). This is how the *Great Bhārata* now relaunches, with a narrative about its first poet; but before he directly addresses the plot of the poem, however, there ensues another lengthy interval devoted to further cosmogony, material which is neither story nor plot but which is essentially 'mythical ancestry'. In one of these micronarratives the tale of Śakuntalā, the mother of the eponymous Bharata, is delivered (I,62–69) and there is also the account of Yayāti, whose sons Yadu and Pūru cause the initial division of clans and the establishment of what became the Yādavas and the Kurus (I,70–89). Yet oddly, in genealogical terms, Yayāti lived before Śakuntalā, so once again there is a temporal disjunction of narrative as the story of the latter is given *before* that of the former.

The Ādi *parvan* is replete with so many small narrative contradictions of this nature, and it is as if this material has been ceremoniously prefixed in an editorial fashion long *after* the work of Vyāsa and his student, Vaiśaṃpāyana, had completed their labours.

At I,90,50 there is a return to the origins of the Hāstinapura family with the tale of Śaṃtanu, the father of Bhīṣma, and thereafter comes another quick summary of the clan which concludes with Janamejaya's offspring. Slowly the poem – once again – begins to circumscribe the elder generations of Bhīṣma and Satyavatī and the subsequent births of Dhṛtarāṣṭra and Pāṇḍu. It is at this point that the character of Vyāsa begins to play a role as an autonomous persona in the poem, as we have depicted in the previous chapter: he now becomes an actor and autonomous agent in his own right (I,99,21). Thence the poem sets out and speaks of the regency of Bhīṣma.[4] It is telling that the epic does not truly commence until Vyāsa actually *enters* the narrative not as creator but as character.

Once again the epic reverts to describing the youthful period in the life of the Pāṇḍavas and their subsequent espousal to Draupadī, as the narrative moves with its habitual back and forth and almost *contrapuntal* impetus, telling and retelling. Only with the entry of Karṇa into the poem at I,181 and then with the entry of Kṛṣṇa at I,183 does the narrative possess the necessary impulse and drive that takes it towards the imminent *bheda* caused by the faulty *rājasūya* and by the consequent fraudulent gaming.

So much narrative dissonance, recursion and at times rational discord of these two poets – the nameless and anonymous figure and the person of Ugraśravas – speaks of how, even in that early period of Vyāsa's original

4 In McGrath, 2018b, ch. 1, I analysed these early years of Bhīṣma's life.

composition, the work was already becoming fragmented and its plot dispersed among many other kinds of narration and perhaps even among geographically localized or dissimilar if not competing clan traditions. It is as if the editors intended to deliver as many possible variant origins and summaries of the poem as they could, drawing from as many traditions as possible that ascribed to the epic poetry of Vyāsa.

Chapter 6

CLOSURE

KṚṢṆA DVAIPAYANA VYĀSA, as a poet, character, prophet and near-divinity, is – as I have demonstrated – an acutely polymorphic and multitextual figure in the *Great Bhārata*. One wonders how it was that the poets who worked in the composition of this epic poem came to understand such an omni-dimensional persona, for there are no obvious models to my present knowledge whose outline influenced those unknown original poets. Vyāsa's matchless presence in the *Great Bhārata* collapses so many diverse figures of narrative causality and combines numerous and multiple temporal influences into the poem that it is almost impossible for the close reader to disengage or infer a finite identity for this character simply from the work.

It is telling that in the absence of Vyāsa, as in the Ādi *parvan*, there is an obvious tradition *about* him even at that preliminary stage of the poem's development: poets were able to speak about him and depict his accomplishments as a *tradition*, for he had already moved beyond the condition of being an arch-poet as well as a mentally or spiritually heroic figure in the text. There is no *synopsis* as to this poetic lore, however, as we just observed in the previous chapter, but only a body of variants.

In a similar vein there is the like example of divine Athena in the Homeric Odyssey – as we shall review in the following chapter – who translates between the immortal world of unearthly speech acts bringing narrative causality to humanity and the mortal world of perpetually changing individuality. I strongly doubt if knowledge of that poem was available to Indian poets of the late Bronze Age, however.

The purpose of comparative methodology or of such a manner of close reading is not merely to indicate communal sources of inspiration but to illustrate the possible manner in which human consciousness can be diversely displayed. Both the Homeric Odyssey and Epic *Mahābhārata* disclose how it was that supernatural agency might participate and influence human accomplishment and the likely justice of worldly achievement. Let us quickly remember that the late Bronze Age world of this heroic literature was absolutely non-secular and therefore completely *unlike* our modernist and contemporary world where scientific and objective principles of efficiency exist. The understanding of those ancient poets of both the universal and natural world was totally different from how it is that we Cartesian moderns might perceive and conceive of the cosmos and its earthly being as a wholly rational system.

In this book we have described and portrayed four levels or conditions of narrative. Firstly, as we have seen, the *Great Bhārata* is a work of art that derives from different phases of production where the effort of both inspiration and edition conduce to different proportions or measurements of Vyasa's poem.

Secondly, the epic projects a most ancient poetic tradition that has strong and compellingly various Āryan springs.

Thirdly, there is the paradoxical character and presence of Vyāsa himself within the narration of the epic, where his identity is a figure of practical intervention, of prediction and of efficacious speech acts. It is as if author Virgil were to appear in the Aeneid as *dramatis persona* and then behave in a causal and active manner in order to manipulate the plot. Or, it is as if a director of a play, having written the script, were then to participate in the drama or filming of the play as a key figure in the momentary development of narration. As part of this manner Vyāsa is also, in an indescribable fashion, a character of mysterious and exclusive communication, one of unique and secret quality and one that is inexplicably composed and interleaved within the plot and only evident to inference.

Finally, the *ṛṣi* soon came to own a polyvalent tradition which surrounded and conveyed many – and at times agonistic – aspects of poetic accomplishment. Our analysis of the opening section of the Ādi *parvan* revealed this dimension.

His name, *Vy-āsa*, the 'one who divides', is telling, for such is the profound and intrinsic attribute of his own and personable nature in the *Great Bhārata.*[1] As we shall soon see, of all the figures in the Āryan tradition of epic poetry that I am presently aware of, it is Athena in the Homeric Odyssey who approximates most closely to this kind of literary formation, where narrative creativity and agency are simultaneously aligned and efficient. She too makes constant pragmatic *divisions* in the weaving of the plot.

Vyāsa's first words within the poem, *smṛto'haṃ darśayiṣyāmi*, 'remembered, I shall cause myself to be seen', are thoroughly indicative of how this currency occurs in the Bhārata Song, for thus 'remembered', the poem appears

1 Herodotus, in his *Histories*, writes of the Homeric tradition in a similar fashion, saying that the names, influence and forms of the deities were established by this epic poetry (II,53,401). That is, it is the poets who *make* the known cosmogony, nomenclature and ceremonial praxis for a culture.

and is performed by poets even today. Yet it is also 'remembered' by the other characters in the poem or is thought of by them: for being remembered causes Vyāsa to appear in whatever scene such thoughts occur.

This is also how Ugraśravas works, when he remembers what he had heard on an earlier occasion and which he reiterates in the Naimiṣa forest. Vaiśaṃpāyana, too, remembers what he had heard at an earlier event and he repeats that. Such verbal recollection causes the poem to become expressed, in speech, in writing and nowadays in digital format on different kinds of screen. There are also, of course, the many millions of sculptural and printed visual images which are drawn from the poem's characters and events that, similarly remembered, often possess and communicate moral truth.

This act of recollection is a cognitive activity and peculiar to each individual who is performing the remembrance, hence the multitudinous range and assortment of interpretations, as we observed in the narrative of the Ādi *parvan*, for instance.

In Chapter 2 I demonstrated how differently the poets and the editors of the *Great Bhārata* worked as they recalled and projected this poetic memory of the two clans who feuded together in dreadful enmity. In Chapter 3 I illustrated what the poets who composed Vyāsa might have heard and 'remembered' about social and cultural situations in the late Bronze Age of North-West India. In Chapter 4, Vyāsa the persona is definitely the vital element in the literal narration of the epic's plot, and this has been the central focus of the present book. His presence in the *story*, as with the long micronarrative about his son Śuka, is curiously ancillary.

In this view, the plot, as I have shown, is arguably a work of primary inspiration, whereas the story is generally the work of edition; and in terms of *phase*, the former precedes the latter. In Chapter 5 we closely read the aspects and qualities of an incipient Vyāsīd tradition and observed numerous versions of those poetic conventions and literary customs respecting the genius of this great *ṛṣi*.

What those early poets were conceiving of as they sang the *Great Bhārata*, as their imagined creator of the work participated in the plot and story as an active and directing character, is presently difficult to infer and apprehend. We might consider the poem a complete ritual in itself and the figure of Vyāsa as the generative *brāhmaṇa* who plays a director's role in the perfection of right continuity in an ongoing series of three rites: a royal ceremony of anointment, a ritual of battle and the extensive ceremonial sacrifice of a horse.[2]

---

2 See McGrath, 2017a, for an analysis of these three rites which are foundational to the narrative of the poem.

Vyāsa in this light would be the character who constantly balances the narrative that encloses and sustains these rites, perpetually remedying any slight deviation which occurs from the correct ritual sequence. The failure of the *rājasūya*, however, causes the eventual demise of the whole clan.

Yet it is difficult for us to understand what the ancient poets had in mind when the character of Vyāsa was being developed as an undying and omniscient poet and prophet who abandoned his own family lineage in favour of benefitting the Yādava people, for Vyāsa translates between so many worlds and epochs and there is an irreducible complexity about his nature. Ultimately, he must remain inconceivable if not uncannily chthonic in nature.

Kṛṣṇa Dvaipāyana, known as Vyāsa, or more popularly now in this twenty-first century as simply the Hindu *Vedvyās*, continues to mature and develop among many genres of folklore, literature, cinema and television, and in innumerable visual fashionings throughout various pictorial and sculptural media. His timeless but not changeless longevity continues to regenerate the *Great Bhārata* tradition amid countless old and new manifestations. The figure of the Vedic Āryan *ṛṣi* who transmitted those most ancient warrior songs about conflict within a family and the ensuing partition of a peopled landscape continues to remain a vital source of commentary upon the experience, emotions and moral universe of contemporary India. Let us now, as a complement to all the above, briefly mention three of these popular renderings of the most creative and most renowned of Indian poets.

In his book *The Great Indian Novel*, Shashi Tharoor portrays Vedvyas with the title of VV-ji, who as an old man in his late eighties dictates his memoirs. Tharoor bases his character on a range of merged historical figures who played significant roles during the struggle for independence and the Quit India Movement.[3] These include C. Rajagopalachari, Sanjeeva Reddy, Acharya Kripani and V. V. Giri, all of whom were influential in the formation of the new republic. Thus Tharoor captures and well represents the deeply *polytropic* nature of the ancient figure of Vyāsa. In this personal narrative, VV-ji is both narrator and a character in the prose whom the other characters address and with whom they enter into dialogue. Tharoor has thus well pictured the intrinsic double nature of epic Vyāsa and imitated that epic form in his modern volume.

Karthika Nair, in her brilliantly feminist twenty-first-century retelling of the poem, makes Satyavatī the core narrative voice of her work. She says, 'Listen: memory, slow yet luminescent, then opened like shafts from an ancient sun. Vyaasa.'[4] 'Vyaasa, my wild, impetuous son – who would, one day, grow

3 Tharoor, 1989.
4 Nair, 2015, p. 82.

into the essence of wisdom, into the mild, omniscient person whose words would be intoned till eternity by men.'[5] Satyavatī says of her prophetic child, 'I could hear truth, many-armed, cruel-tongued, singing through Vyaasa's voice. But why, I asked in despair, could he not obviate the course of history with all his astral powers, why did he not erase this hate [...]?' To this her son responds, 'Mother, I cannot invent the story. The story invented itself, invented you and me. I can merely act as a channel, an implement. I am assigned to circulate the epic in the world.'[6] It is thus that Nair recognizes and replays this supratemporal quality of the ancient *ṛṣi* and also the cosmic and supernal nature of the *Great Bhārata* for it is *the* poem of all India.

Girja Kumar, in his study of the *Mahābhārata*, also echoes this view of the polyvalent *ṛṣi* when he portrays Vyāsa as 'the cat with nine lives'.[7] He perceives the paradoxical charisma of this character when he comments on the vast extent of the poem, saying that the text 'attributed to Vyasa did not contain a single word directly credited to him. He makes sudden appearance, but he also vanishes in no time leaving no traces [...] He also pervades the entire thought process of the MBh.'[8]

Nowadays Vyāsa is believed by many if not most of the Indian population, both metropolitan and rural, to have *written* the complete poem as it exists and is known in the twenty-first century, and this is what I would consider as most truly the new situation of Vyāsa *redux* where the *ṛṣi* as poet has become the author of what is nowadays known as the *foundation myth* of contemporary India, so in effect denying three millennia of human entropy.

Vyāsa continues to be honoured in the contemporary Hindu calendar on the occasion of *Guru Pūrṇimā*, the full-moon day during the month of Āṣāḍha, that is, at some time during Western June–July.

The method of analysis that we have pursued in the course of this work has been one of *close reading* of the poem. This is not philology but a critical process of slow and lapidary attention to the repetition of specific words in a text. Let us summarily review five aspects of this practice.

Firstly, studying how the same word or phrase is repeatedly utilized by the poets and how it functions in terms of the semantic field that is generated is the primary work of a close reader, one that is revealing of hidden and implicit connections.

Secondly, what is happening within the mental awareness and the emotional or affective situation of characters – aspects of a person which are not

5 Ibid., p. 104.
6 Ibid., p. 206.
7 Kumar, 2016, p. 123. These 'words', I presume, refer to the PCE.
8 Ibid.

vocalized – offer another line of approach for the close reader. Such occurs when a character perceives in another character or in that person's speech something which is not explicitly expressed and yet which influences how the narrative moves. Or, there are unspoken emotions which a character experiences and which similarly have consequence in the plot's evolution: these are to be noted by the close reader and their meaning inferred. Such recognitions and notices only derive from a nuanced reading of what can be lightly described as a character's *mind*: phenomena that the poets are aware of but which the reader must focus his or her attention upon if they are to observe what is only psychically occurring and not overtly or literally represented. These occasions and indications are never unequivocally articulated and are solely available to inference, an inference that is only founded on the perception of exacting evidence, for this is not a process of empathy.

Thirdly, there is also a tertiary action, that of the interstitial analysis of such social institutions as kinship structures and political and economic systems which as human or ethnographic formations are submerged in the poetry and are not immediately obvious. These patterns of the social are presumed by the poets, and in Chapter 3 we touched upon a few of these designs or configurations. The close reader needs to be able to associate small moments of evidence with other brief yet *like* instances and so develop an inferential model that enables him or her to be able to reconstruct what is implied and implicit within those ethnographic, political and economic systems. This necessitates a certain *ethnographie de texte*, or an archaeological approach to the stratification of a literature.

Fourthly, in terms of close reading approaches, anatomy is not destiny and we cannot presume that what occured between the male and the feminine in late Bronze Age society is identical to twenty-first-century habits, bonds and marital contracts. Preliterate and premonetary North-West Indian culture is profoundly *unlike* what we understand as the culture of the subcontinent today, and only by careful and detailed close reading of the poem can we begin to infer and then to perceive details about how amicable life and connubial society were organized in those ancient days.

Fifthly, the mnemonic skills of the poets are unlike how contemporary literary artists work with and recall language, and these too are only to be apprehended by slow and rigorous reading, which might identify those technical manners and skills. How did those ancient poets *call to mind* their work, and what cognitive techniques were involved in this process of mental retrieval?

In all my books the art of close reading has been a consistent and completely empirical method of analysis, and different books have focused on varying topics and themes of research: the ancient Āryan ideal of the hero, the nature of the feminine and its multiple nuptial forms, modes of poetic inspiration and recollection, Bronze Age charioteering, the polities of archaic kingship and preliterate and premonetary economy, and the formation of poetic and moral authority, to name a few subjects. I have always been interested in the culture and society represented by the *Great Bhārata* rather than by the immediate formations of its grammar, syntax and nomenclature, and I have paid constant attention to understanding how it is that this poetry was long ago performed and how it *worked* in late antiquity, both for the poets and for a hypothetical audience.

In sum, let us say that narrative, in one sense, is the sequencing of information, one which utilizes mnemonic systems and their known anterior elements so enabling an efficient process of speaking. As we have seen, the *maharṣi* Vyāsa is a master, *the* master of creativity when the metaphors of the epic poem were initially established and its matrix introduced. Then, as a prismatic and certainly pre-Cartesian presence within the work, he demonstrates a most dominant expertise with metonymy, always sustaining the movement of the narrative along whatever trajectory is selected or foreseen. The production, transmission and continual reception of this sequence, as expressed by Epic *Mahābhārata*, has been the focus of this book.

Chapter 7

HOMERIC ODYSSEUS

ODYSSEUS the hero and king is portrayed in the Homeric epic as a type of what it means to be *polytropic*, the fifth word of the poem and a word which only occurs on one other occasion when Circe welcomes him to her isle at x,331.[1] It is not simply his character, however, but also the medium of poetry and the narrative itself which is polytropic, for there are four fundamental modes of the journey of Odysseus, courses which supply differing kinds of awareness and temporal dimension to his person; about these models varying periods of time are attached.

What follows is a brief complement to what we have examined in the complex narrative form and edifice as delivered to us by the poets who composed the *Mahābhārata* narrative from a larger and more comparative perspective.[2] This chapter develops the conceptual model which we lightly portrayed in Chapter 3.

In Epic *Mahābhārata* more than half of the poem is essentially set at Kurukṣetra, either as a place of battle or as a place of oration; the rest of the narrative concerns other locations. The *Great Bhārata* demonstrates a density and convolution of narrative form or mode just as throughout the Odysseus poem the common unities of time are not observed in any degree at all: what exists are narrative *structures*, not sequences. This is what I would assert as being, for mnemonic purposes, transitions which once assisted the poets in their work. Only during the four Kurukṣetra Books is there any iteration of days presented, 18 of them; otherwise human time in the Sanskrit epic's narrative is not a significant element of the poem; it is a vague and insubstantial quality, that is all.

---

1 I am extremely grateful to my friend and colleague Aldo Bottino, who shared with me some of his close readings of the many competing narratives of heroic Odysseus. I am also deeply grateful to Gregory Nagy for his comments on this chapter.

2 The poem, when not being given in open narrative form, is generally composed of duets between two speakers: Zeus and Athena, Hermes and Calypso, Odysseus and various interlocutors, for instance. Duet is the usual mode of direct poetic speech in the Odyssey.

This supernumerary chapter directs our attention to the extraordinary narrative complexity of the Homeric Odyssey and, unlike the Homeric Iliad, there is no simple narrative constitution which accounts for the hero during an integral series of days.[3] The intricacy with which the plot is organized is akin to the vast canvas which the *Great Bhārata* presents, in terms of how the plot moves and the enormous amount of story which is attached to it. Let us now examine the narrative order of this Homeric poem as a counter-illustration which can fruitfully mirror the multifarious movements of the *Great Bhārata*. For us, as modern close readers, such compound narration offers a specific communication in which narrative form itself becomes ultimately metaphorical.

The cosmic economy of the Homeric epic is fundamentally composed of three systems: putative human volition, rituals of blood sacrifice, and divine action and direction.[4] This is how the mortal and supernal worlds function together, and there is a constant circulation between these registers wherein prophecy sometimes mediates and connects the hierarchies.[5] This economy

---

3 Time in the poem can be roughly calibrated as follows: Scrolls i–iv, 6 days; v–xii, 28 days, within which ix–xii make up an interior nine years, seven of which are with Calypso; xiii–xxiv, 6 days, and within that there is xxiii,310–43, representing nine years. These periods of course are not in any timely succession – one does not follow another; rather, they are dimensions of temporal perspective. The overall master narrative thus occupies about 40 days, which is akin to the overarching master narrative of Homeric Iliad.

4 Apollo has a favourable relation with Odysseus; it is the festival of Apollo when the archery contest is held in Scroll xxi, and in Scroll I of the Homeric Iliad, Odysseus sponsors a formal sacrifice towards Apollo. He also says that he had once visited Delos (vi,162). Odysseus conducts several other rituals as at ix,231, and at ix,532 Odysseus sacrifices to Zeus and there is also an altar dedicated to Zeus in his palace on Ithaca. At i,60–2 Athena reminds Zeus about how frequently Odysseus used to perform rites for him whilst at Troy. In Scroll Eleven, Odysseus sacrifices to Hades and Persephone, and later, he is instructed to sacrifice to Poseidon when his life approaches closure. In Scroll Two there is actually an annual sacrifice to Poseidon which is being sponsored by Nestor, in which both Telemachus and Athena participate; in classical times this calendrical event occurred during the midwinter months, for which see Parke, 1977.

5 Prophecy connects differing moments in the narrative movement but in an irrational or atemporal fashion. One can see this in the *Great Bhārata* with the words of Vyāsa or of Nārada, and such verbal proceedings or occasions supply internal strength to a complex narrative reticulation. Prophecy in the Homeric Odyssey happens when Zeus predicts the events in the narrative of Odysseus at v,29; this passage replicates the dialogue of Athena and Zeus in Scroll One – it is recursive. Zeus at i,35 tells of how, in a message, he had predicted the deaths of Aegisthus and Agamemnon. The Cyclops at ix,512 mentions a prophecy whereby Odysseus would arrive and cause his blindness, and at x,331 there is a prophecy about Odysseus landing on the isle of Circe; similarly, the Sirens know that it is Odysseus who approaches their isle in Scroll Twelve. Theoclymenus prophesies the vengeful return of Odysseus at xvii,155, and such forecasts connect the narrative with an outer frame of imperative, one which is often apart even from the principal and driving

obversely entails a sometimes *lack* of right human volition and a lack of right sacrifice, both of which play into this universal system but with negative import.

The four fundamental narratives depicting Odysseus which illustrate this situation are the following: The overall and master narrative of the poem itself in 24 scrolls. Then, there is the present narrative of Scrolls Five to Eight, which describes the hero alone and without crew, who moves across the sea assisted by the mentoring deity Athena. Beyond this movement there is the past micronarrative performed by Odysseus himself, which occurs in Scrolls Nine to Twelve; here Odysseus is in the company of his crews and is without guidance from Athena. Lastly, in Scroll xxiii, from line 310 onwards, there is a brief summary portrayal, spoken by the hero to his wife as they lie abed before sleep, in which he tells retrospectively of the complete journey, from Troy towards the island of Ithaca.

There are also many small internal instants of textual counterpoint, as when Telemachus – having travelled from Ithaca – meets Helen in Scroll iv, whilst Odysseus is at that moment arriving on the island having previously left Helen at Troy. Also, Ithaca is said to be an isle unfit for horses, unlike Troy, which is famed for its equines and equestrians. When Odysseus enters his own domain he is dressed as a beggar, just as when he entered the city of Troy he wore the impoverished and distressed clothing of a mendicant (iv,244–51). Likewise, the Phaeacians live in a purely timeless world that is akin to the land of the Cyclops, and in fact, both peoples once lived together (vi,4–9 and vii,207). Finally, just before the king and his wife retire to bed for the first time in 19 years, the simile that the poets utilize is one where Penelope is a vessel being driven by stormy Poseidon and Odysseus is the land upon which the surviving mariners find life – which is a nice reversal of all previous imagery concerning Odysseus (xxiii,233–40). Such are just a few brief instants of inherent counterpoint in the poem, and in a like fashion of narrative symmetry Odysseus's time on Ithaca occupies the second half or hemisphere of the work. These kinds or instances of duality are what I would aver as being mnemonic devices in the art of the poets, small systems which facilitate the performance of the work or how the poem *came to mind* during presentation.

The basic terrestrial diagram of the poem would be: Troy > Isle of Cyclops > Calypso > Phaeacia > Ithaca, with Calypso in the central and focal position and the other four situations diametrically grouped. These are the places which – apart from what the audience hear during Scrolls

---

speech acts of Zeus. Concerning the bird auguries which Helen and then Theoclymenus interpret, it is as if the natural world is actually reflecting a reverse impulse from what will become the future narrative (xiv,172 and xv,531).

Nine to Twelve – occupy the master narrative and which are indicated by Zeus and Athena at the outset of the work. The ruling family of Phaeacia is – like the Cyclops – descended from Poseidon and, when Odysseus arrives and departs from Ogygia, the isle of Calypso, he is shipwrecked on both occasions thus stylistically emphasizing this modelling of Cyclops > Calypso > Phaeacia.

Also, in the discourse of Zeus and Athena these five locations are the only ones to be mentioned as being places on the journey of the hero and king. This is the core narrative of the poem, but it is one whose description is dispersed throughout the epic so that the plot is not overtly expressed but discreet within the story, just as a human skeleton is hidden by tissue and flesh.

For instance, Calypso is mentioned 34 times during the course of the Odyssey, and it is as if she is the critical and original source for the travels of Odysseus; her island is the *omphalós*, the 'navel' of the poem (i,50).[6] In the same way, Vyāsa too, in that he originates with a speech act the hypothetical source of the *Great Bhārata* at the snake sacrifice of *rāja* Janamejaya at Takṣaśilā, is in an identical focal or pivotal position. Both Vyāsa's proto-poem performed at that initial rite and Calypso's isle not only mark the original point of departure for the respective works, but both are actual figures in the corresponding poems which the poets repeatedly mention as if they are landmarks or mnemonic beacons. Neither poem actually commences with these original moments or places of the narrative sequence, however, for they paradoxically occur only after the launch of the work.

I would argue that such elaborate and heterogeneous poetic formation is not simply a means of communicating a structured body of information but is also a medium of *aide-mémoire* – one that is structural rather than simply temporal – by which the poets were able to work with a prodigious mass of traditional poetry during a preliterate and premonetary period. Having these narrative *periods* to work with allowed the poets to bring involution to their art; this is not the case with the Heracles poem, the Argonautica or the Rāmāyaṇa, all of which follow a single temporal series of events.

Let us now recount the distinct fashioning of Odyssean narrative and observe how this kind of plot and story reflect upon the narrative patterns of the cognate *Great Bhārata*; that is, what can the former can tell us about the latter?

---

6 In the Hesiodic Theogony, 1011–15, it is said that both Circe and Calypso bore sons to Odysseus. Odysseus is here unlike other mortals who come into tactile or sexual contact with divinities, for usually this presages death for the human. Likewise, this hero is unlike all other mortals, as he is the only one to visit and return from Hades, alive and reminiscent.

As with the commencement of the *Mahābhārata*, there is a voice other than the narrator which precedes the opening of the literal poem; here, in the Greek epic the poet addresses the Muse, requesting that she tell of the *versatile* hero. He cues her by mentioning the island of Thrinacia, and immediately at line 11 the Muse commences the song by responding to the prompt and by beginning her narration with the statement that Odysseus was on the isle of Calypso: for it was after Thrinacia that Odysseus lost his final crew and then washed up solo upon the shore of Calypso's terrain. This is situated somewhere between Scylla and Charybdis and the isle of the Sirens. She also says that it was the anger of Poseidon that delayed the hero's *nostos* or 'return'. This is how the Muse commences her work, mentioning two principle motifs that recur throughout the telling of the Odyssey: Calypso and Poseidon.

There are seven narrative *periods* during the narration of Odysseus in the poem, each of which offers a different dimension or perspective of the hero's travelling, a journey that is not so much geographical but *conscient* or conceptual; that is, one which concerns the movement of his consciousness and how it is that the *nóos* or 'mentality' of Odysseus becomes integrated into that of a psychically coherent individual. In that sense, the narrative is a metaphor of all that goes to constitute and compose human awareness, implying that consciousness is formulated of diverse narrative events which become cognitively united. As with the travails of Heracles or the voyage of Jason and his Argonaut crew, the 12 stations on the way are not so much geographical as mental and emotional, and in the case of Odysseus, these stages are nearly always meditated by women, by speech that is feminine.[7]

There is no simple temporal sequence between these periodic aspects of the narrative, and sometimes the movement of the poem moves forward whilst at other times it is analeptic or in *flashback* form. Narrative structure is here what I would assert as being employed by the poets as a system of mental stimuli rather than as a temporal narration that is ideally serial, for not only is there a steady disjunction of time but the perspective of these separate narrations is also taken from different angles and persons. Only at the end, when Odysseus sums up all his travels for his wife as they lie together in bed having just made love, is there any comprehensive and integrated serial transition to be found, and then, much is omitted from the telling in terms of its causality. For at that point King Odysseus is in complete command of his life's agency and its effects, a coherence that only becomes available at the resolution of the overall cycle. Having become master of his own narrative, he can now ignore events which impinged upon his journey with such terrific necessity; now he pretends

---

7 For Heracles, see Diodorus of Sicily IV,11,3–IV,26,4. For the Argonautica, see Apollodorus.

that they never occurred and that only Odysseus is and was both complete director and master narrator. His audience, Penelope, is, of course, unconditionally attuned to her poet.

The initial period of narration occurs during the opening four scrolls of the poem, which render many varying and cursory accounts given of Odysseus and his time at Troy. The deity Athena is the first to name Odysseus, she being then in colloquy with Zeus, who owns the first voice in the poem; they are discussing the situation of the hero (i,48). Athena proposes that Hermes be sent to command Calypso to direct Odysseus homewards, and Athena informs Zeus that she will oversee Telemachus's journey towards the Pylos of old Nestor; this is tacitly affirmed by Zeus, and so, the initial speech act of these deities establishes the plot of the master narrative: that Odysseus should depart from Ogygia and return towards Ithaca (i,82, and referred to by Poseidon at xiii,131–33).[8]

It is at the point when Athena appears on Ithaca that natural time or mortal time, which is just one component of narrative time, commences at i,113. She identifies herself as Mentes and tells of her friendship with Odysseus in words that are 'untrue' and fabricated: this is how the poem commences, via the medium of fiction or fallacy. Then she begins to advise and direct young Telemachus in the process of his Telemachy, and in the guise of Mentor she reappears on the evening of the second day and again specifically directs him (ii,270–95).[9]

At this point many succinct mentions of Odysseus are given by Telemachus, Athena, Phemios, Penelope, Aegyptios, Halitherses, Eurymachos, Mentor, Leiocritos, Eurycleia, Nestor, Menelaos, Helen and Proteus, and they tell of the *kléos* of the warrior and thus the audience hear of that earlier and martial time of his life. This is the first dimension of Odysseus's narrative, where his heroic past is described for its 'fame' through *hearsay* and retrospection.

---

8 The poem opens and closes with an exchange being made between Zeus and Athena, and similarly in the Homeric Iliad the poem begins and concludes with a verbal exchange between Zeus and Thetis. Both of these exchanges, in the Homeric Iliad and Odyssey, establish the basis of the plot; in the former this is categorized as the 'will of Zeus', what is in effect the 'anger' of Achilles translated via a speech act by the deity into what amounts to the overall narrative (I,528). In the latter it is the speech acts of Athena and Zeus which launch the plot. Let us recall that the patriline of Odysseus's family descends from Arkeisios, who in turn is descended from Zeus (xiv,182).

9 She also directs him at i,420–24 and ii,14–28, and at ii,382–87 she actually impersonates Telemachus and recruits men for his voyage towards mainland Peloponissos. In Scroll Fifteen she again appears to the young prince, this time in his dream, and tells him to depart from Sparta and also to beware of the suitors who are waiting to kill him.

The second transition or narrative period occurs when Odysseus actually makes his entry into the poem at the outset of Scroll Five, where he first appears sitting on the shore and is weeping in remembrance of Penelope; this takes place on Ogygia, the isle of Calypso, and marks a second order of narration. At this point the poets are making a reversal in time, for earthly or poetic time – the temporal period of the master narrative – has returned to that point in Scroll One where Zeus was about to commission Hermes to visit Calypso. The five days contained in the first four scrolls are thus apparently cancelled or inverted as the poem begins anew, although Athena does say that Telemachus was then present at Sparta. There is an indistinct blurring of two narrative sequences here, perhaps because worldly and diurnal time is unlike heavenly and immortal time, and it is irrational to attempt to correlate precisely the two kinds of chronology.

Odysseus has been on this island for seven years, and he is seen alone and without his men and is in the same immediate time as the audience: this is neither past nor future. Only in Scroll Nine does the audience begin to hear – from the retrospective words and narration of Odysseus himself – about how the hero fared when he was formerly accompanied by his initial 12 crews and vessels.

Scroll Five commences with a second dialogue between Zeus and Athena, in which Zeus describes how Odysseus will return towards his isle, so establishing the narrative of the next eight scrolls with his speech act (v,28–42).[10] Zeus also tells of how Athena had been planning for the warrior to return to his island kingdom and to take his revenge (v,23–24). Odysseus – the hero now appearing as a technician – constructs his own craft from island timber using an axe, an adze and an auger.[11] His voyage towards Phaeacia continues for 17 days until he is wrecked by a wave sent by Poseidon and then he languishes in the water; a sea nymph, Ino, offers him succour and Athena redirects the winds and drives him towards his next destination (v,382). This instant is the only actual – rather than reported – occasion where the deity Poseidon actively delays the return of our hero.

Athena once more participates in the narrative as a character – disguised as always – and directs the young princess Nausikaa towards where Odysseus

10 The force of Zeus's projection of the Odyssean narrative is later witnessed – in terms of augury – by Helen and Menelaos in Scroll iv and by the *mantis* Theoclymenus at xv,172, xv,531 and xx,351. The narrative thus possesses a certain external or cosmic drive, something auxiliary to what is simply occurring *within* the plot. This narrative connection between Zeus and Odysseus is affirmed by the latter's invocation at xx,98.

11 Trees are an important signifier in the poem, and a great variety of them are specifically mentioned: they are always *indicators*.

has landed. Athena immediately reappears in another semblance and this time actually instructs the hero himself, telling him how to find the palace of Alcinous (vii,27); there he must supplicate Queen Arete, who is descended from Poseidon (vii,56). At last in the presence of King Alcinous, Odysseus narrates how he had arrived on the isle of Calypso and later departed thence, until vexed by Poseidon's bad weather he was soon to arrive on Phaeacia. Narrative time is thus moving forwards and backwards, depending on whose voice is delivering the poetry.

That is, in his speech to Queen Arete, to whom he is a suppliant, Odysseus relates his voyage from the moment he became sole, when Zeus struck down his final ship; the first word of this micronarrative is 'Ogygia'. He then tells of his time with Calypso and how it was that he arrived on Phaeacia and thus rehearses what the audience had essentially just heard in the previous two scrolls (vii,245–97).

In this second period, we again observe Zeus initially impelling the narrative with his speech act and then Athena actually participating in the narrative, either supernaturally or in mortal disguise, and conducing to its onward motion. Let us repeat, from an audience point of view, that is, in the outer frame of the plot, that Odysseus is described in the narration as only being on Ogygia, on Phaeacia and, soon, on Ithaca: that is all the audience perceives in the holding narrative. All the other places of his journey are given via internal narration by Odysseus himself in Scrolls Nine to Twelve and in his summary in Scroll Twenty-Three.[12]

There is a transitory third period of narration in Scroll Eight when the ancient poet Demodocus performs two songs which tell of Odysseus: recounting an event which happened before the fighting at Troy and then speaking of events during the sack of Troy itself.[13] The first song speaks of a quarrel between Odysseus and Achilles (viii,75), then later in the day Odysseus himself commissions the poet to sing of the destruction of Troy (viii,492).

These two songs, although they are essentially *story* or further 'hearsay' about the hero, do cause Odysseus to experience extreme grief, and hence he atones for some of the dreadful violence which he had perpetrated, experienced and

12 That is, with the exception of the cursory mention of the destruction and consumption of the cattle of the Helios by the poet who is addressing the Muse at the outset of the poem; the location of this event is not stated. Odysseus himself – in his poem to the Phaeacian court – is the only other voice to tell of these cattle, and he speaks the name of the island at that point. Thus outer poet and Odysseus, the inner poet, are equated, which is a pertinent and telling counterpoint. The Muse does tell of the anger of Poseidon at i,19–21, and Zeus does mention *en passant* the Cyclops at i,69–79.

13 In the *Iliou Persis*, the penultimate summary of Proclus in his Epic Cycle, Odysseus is also described as he acts as a warrior in a thoroughly violent and intransigent manner.

endured; and in this sense the songs – being efficacious in that his trauma is assuaged – can be said to constitute an oblique aspect of the plot concerning how the consciousness of Odysseus advances and develops during the course of the poem. Between the events of these two songs there is an occasion for athletic endeavour during which the prowess of Odysseus is mildly insulted and tested. He responds in a greatly *braggadocio* fashion, boasting about his excellence and how no one at Troy exceeded him in weaponry, except for Philoctetes in archery. He tells the Phaeacians how he was 'the best' of all men at that time (viii,223). This is a rare instance in the poem where Odysseus proclaims and vaunts his superlative nature, and he does so again at ix,20; it is similar in manner to how he says that he spoke with the Cyclops (ix,502). Again, there is this symmetry between Phaeacia and the isle of the Cyclops. Usually the hero is never explicitly open and direct about himself but always guards his words and remains verbally undisclosed; he is generally emotionally veiled.

The fourth period in the Odysseus narrative begins in Scroll Nine when the hero, having announced his name, begins to tell – speaking like an inventive poet – of his travels and voyages; he is addressing the court of Alcinous and he talks in a performative fashion, imitating dozens of different characters in this long personal narrative that continues throughout a highly dramatic four scrolls. Athena had already, the day prior, gone about the town in another of her identities and summoned men of the community to attend the court of Alcinous so that Odysseus would have an audience (viii,7–25).

There are thus three fundamental *speakers* of the overall master poem: the poet who addresses the first 11 lines of the song to the Muse; the Muse who then performs the entire song; and within that, there is now Odysseus himself, who in Scrolls Nine to Twelve sings his own *histoire*, impersonating and imitating the voices of numerous personae.

This narration begins with his departure – a retrojection of nine years – along with 12 boats and crews from Troy, and then describes all his ordeals until he arrives on Phaeacia. Odysseus expounds about the events on the island of the Cyclops and of how the blinded son of Poseidon cursed the hero with a speech act, calling upon his father to cause Odysseus not to reach his destination until all his crews were dead and he needed the conveyance of another vessel (ix,526). These words are effective and so the plot moves to another trajectory, although at the time this shift is not obvious and remains only in potential. Once again it is the speech act of an inhuman force that drives the basic impulse of the narrative or journey. He concludes his narration to the Phaeacian court with another reference to the isle of Calypso.[14]

---

14 There are two small disjunctive moments in this micronarrative of Odysseus: one

Apart from what happens subsequent to the curse of the Cyclops which invokes the wrath of Poseidon, and also this particular mention of Calypso, none of the events in the song of Odysseus have any bearing on the overall or framing plot of the poem, for the reason – so I would argue – that Athena is absent from the song. One might add the interdiction offered by Teiresias in Scroll Eleven in the Underworld concerning the cattle of the Sun as forbidden food, but this is in fact irrelevant as the prohibition is not respected.[15] These four scrolls thus represent what can be termed as *story*.

Insofar as Zeus has – with his speech act – indicated that the Phaeacians will convey Odysseus to his island kingdom, and that Alcinous has already – with another speech act – publically vowed to do this, the lengthy song of Odysseus has no consequence upon the larger enclosing poem except to magnify and amplify the greatness of the hero for enduring terrific trials, including an entry into and retreat from Hades itself. This micronarrative of Scrolls Nine to Twelve is the first occasion when Odysseus gives voice to his own journey, and it is here that he first demonstrates his own unguided volition and moral or intellectual autonomy. Instead of hearsay, now the audience receives knowledge of this hero directly through his own words.[16]

Let us repeat that this is almost all story and is not plot. What one can aver is that it is a portrait of a warrior-hero, Odysseus, as given in his own voice, but this has no bearing upon the narration of his journey, apart from – as we have already observed – the speech act of the Cyclops and the presence of Odysseus on Ogygia.

There is one curious moment in this song of Odysseus where he quotes a dialogue between Zeus and Helios. Cleverly, he tells his audience that this is something which he heard from Calypso, who had heard it from Hermes.

---

occurs when Hermes simply appears – without any obvious cause – before the hero at x,275. The other happens when Circe informs him that he must go to Hades. Both of these instants are without mediate narrative precedent and lack uniformity with what precedes them and it is as if the poem has made an unreasoned shift in disclosure, for the moments lack regular or typical metonymy.

15 Teiresias also knows of the speech act or curse of the Cyclops (xi,100), and he repeats the wording of the Cyclops which was made at x,530 but now connects it with the breach in prohibition concerning the cattle of the Sun, thereby rendering the curse his own speech act and applicable to a different event (xi,110). Circe likewise draws upon these words of the seer, warning Odysseus about the interdiction (xi,139–41). This kind of internal repetition and reticulation of language binds the narrative periods most firmly. Remember also that Odysseus is both the poet and the speaker of all these voices who repeat such statements.

16 The first hemisphere of the poem ends with these *summary* four scrolls, just as the second half of the work similarly concludes in summary form with the small compressed song that commences at xxiii,310.

Such use of report or hearsay by poetic Odysseus himself is unique during these scrolls and amplifies the irrational complexity which binds the elements of the poem into an inclusive unity and compellingly plausible whole (xii,389–90).[17] It also qualifies the authority and verbal consciousness of our hero as advancing towards greater competence and narrative autonomy: *he* is the one to know about what Zeus has been saying.

The fifth period of narration concerns all the second half of the Homeric Odyssey when the hero has at last returned to his kingdom of Ithaca, although his consciousness is such that he does not recognize the land of his kingdom and needs to be informed by Athena as to the place. She calls him *népiós*, 'foolish', for his lack of awareness (xiii,237). Then, until the outset of Scroll Twenty-Two, he remains incognito due to the magic of Athena, for even though he is king his position is generally anonymous until he has caused the death of the 108 suitors. Curiously, at one point Odysseus is uniquely described by the poets as being 'blonde' (xiii,431).

Here, in the second half of the epic, the first occasion occurs where Odysseus appears in a non-supernatural setting, for descriptions of him during the first hemisphere of the poem always portray him in situations that are not completely mortal. These second 12 scrolls are thoroughly natural apart from the intermittent presence and steady direction of Athena and the thunder and lightning-bolt of Zeus in Scroll Twenty-Four. Also, with Scrolls Fourteen and Fifteen, the two narratives of Odysseus and Telemachus at last begin to intersect and conjoin.

Once Odysseus enters the palace in Scroll Seventeen, the dramatic tension of the song suddenly increases as violence begins to develop, at first in terms of insult, provocation and threat, until Scroll Twenty-Two when the killings are made. Even the serene and melancholic Penelope makes a speech act, cursing Antinoos to die from an arrow, and this is of course successful (xvii,493–94). As part of this process of surging emotional tautness, the poets often address Eumaios in the vocative during Scroll Seventeen, which is a most effective way of drawing the audience further into the gathering and charged affect of the drama as it becomes increasingly graphic and immediate.

There are five instances of attentive duplicity in this second half of the poem, verbal occasions when the hero dissembles about his identity: to Athena, to Eumaios, to Antinoos, to Penelope and to his father, although Odysseus does not make any pretence to his son about his personality.[18] To

---

17 These lines were athetized by Aristarchus.

18 To Eumaios, his tale is about Troy and Egypt and is akin to the tale which Menelaos tells Telemachus in Scroll Four, although in the Eumaios story Odysseus spends much more narrative and historical time in Egypt (xiv,99–354). In this fabled account, Odysseus makes use of many events and phrases that have already occurred in his long *histoire* to

Eumaios, Odysseus tells of events at Troy and how he had acted there; when he speaks with Penelope he likewise tells of how he encountered Odysseus in earlier times.[19] So the audience returns to a situation of hearsay, with the rider that the speaker on these occasions is Odysseus himself, disguised and not disclosing his true subjectivity.

In terms of *nóos*, of how the consciousness of Odysseus is operating and becoming aroused, such practical dubiety illustrates an awareness on the part of the hero and his mental capacity for recognizing and displaying the utility of fiction. Consciousness that is able to secure worth from fiction is greater than a consciousness that is limited by known truth or compulsive mendacity.[20]

Athena directs Odysseus as to what he should next do, promising him that the suitors will be eventually killed (xiii,392).[21] Again, the audience perceives how the deity oversees the narrative evolution and how omniscient she is about what is occurring in the poem, just like the omniconscient and predictive Vyāsa. Yet she is always disguised in some mortal envelope and is simultaneously directing the movements of Telemachus as he travels to and from Sparta as well as having oversight in how Penelope behaves and speaks. As with the *Great Bhārata*, the Homeric Odyssey is not simply about a singular hero but about the dynamics of a family and how this social group is 'moved' by divine agency.

Alcinous and his court. Egypt is an important landmark in the narrative of the overall poem and receives more description than Troy itself. Odysseus also tells another tale to the swineherd about an event at Troy in which Odysseus appears, described in the third person (xiv,462). Let us recall that Odysseus's maternal grandfather, Autolycus, was famed for theft and deceit (xix,396), and conversely and as a rider to this, both Arete and Alcinous publicly question the veracity of what Odysseus has been telling them 'like a poet', yet they are keen to continue listening to his amazing song (xi,336–37 and 362–76). Similarly, Eumaios tells Odysseus not to be 'dishonest' in his accounts (xiv,386).

19 The poets themselves refer to his *pseúdea*, 'deceit', at xix,203.

20 In Hesiodic Theogony even the Muses – whose consciousness or awareness is absolute – are said to know how 'to speak *pséudea*, "deceit", like the truth' (26).

21 The theme of guest–host relations is constantly iterated throughout the poem; that is, how important for the plot is the goodness of both guest and host as they accomplish the correct reciprocal protocols of hospitality, and when these rules of commensality are not sustained the plot or story becomes thoroughly disordered. The first scene in the Homeric Odyssey in an earthly temporal setting is one of equable communal dining (i,136). This theme is akin to how the degradation of Draupadī in the Sabhā *parvan* completely destabilizes the kingdom, as does the disordering of propriety in the *rājasūya* rite when Śiśupāla is decapitated. Right protocol is not simply social but is also an important dynamic in the causal order of poetic narration; it is metaphor pointing at how the narrative is either presenting right or wrong conduct.

Meanwhile, there is often declaration of and allusion to Odysseus in these scrolls by Eumaios, by the suitors, by Telemachus and by Penelope, and his name is constantly passed – like currency – throughout the palace scenes; even Odysseus, masquerading as he is, tells stories about his fictional past. This hearsay simultaneously activates differing views and aspects of Odysseus for the audience and is a constant subtext in the poem making the *past* Odysseus actually *present*, for the two kinds of narrative now combine. Also, during this final quarter of the poem, by invocation and by recollection, the presence of Zeus in the life of Odysseus becomes more pronounced and intimate as the narrative which has been generated by the speech act of Zeus comes to conclusive fruition. The audience perceives how, in the ritual economy of sacrifice, devotion and blood ceremonies actually *do* activate the particular deity who is being addressed and there then occurs a significant divine reciprocity. The suitors, of course, never perform any ritual action.[22]

Soon, in Scroll Seventeen, the king-hero himself appears at the *mégaron*, 'palace', moving closer and closer towards Penelope in the veneer of an old vagabond, and thus the long final scene of the epic commences during which time Odysseus has verbal exchanges with various members of the suitors, the household and field staff. Repeatedly, there are these small incidents, verbal 'snapshots' of the hero in brief and testy communication.

Thus, simultaneously there are three 'characters' functioning at once: the Odysseus of hearsay, the Odysseus in disguise and Odysseus disclosed who engages with Telemachus and Athena and later with a few of his domestic people. Again, such is the extensive polytropic quality of our hero, but, as we have argued, this is an emblem of the marvellous versatility of the narrative itself and its many dimensional periods.

Then occurs the magnificent slow recognition scene in Scroll Nineteen where Odysseus and Penelope twice interview each other in enigmatic terms, neither proclaiming their true emotional awareness nor revealing any overt intimacy. This instant culminates on the next day with the archery contest – proposed by Penelope, who by now appears to have guessed the identity of the surreptitious vagrant – and the merciless death of the suitors, 12 servant women, and a goatherd who is mutilated and left to haemorrhage fatally. After the mayhem there is another scene where king and queen try each other verbally until, at last convinced of each other's love and also of their blameless

22 Sacrifice is of course another aspect of cosmic commensality, or what some would call a *sacrificial cuisine*, the three nutrients being smoke, cooked meat and blood, which sustain the tripartite registry of the cosmos: aerial deities, terrestrial mortals and subterranean deceased heroes.

mutual consciousness, they kiss and retire to their inimitable and climactic bedchamber.[23]

In the penultimate event of the poem where the deceased suitors speak together in Hades with Agamemnon and Achilles about what Odysseus had done to them, Achilles is silent during these moments and only Agamemnon responds.[24] Thus the poem comes to its terminus with the hero being named and discussed in the Underworld, hearsay being the medium of expression once more, but by this time the audience themselves are privy to the reports, having actually *witnessed* them in the preceding scrolls; so it is at this moment that the audience themselves participate, albeit mutely, in the accounts.

Finally in Scroll Twenty-Four, Odysseus meets with his father and they dine together, just as in the Homeric Iliad the poem closes with Achilles meeting with Priam in a commensal situation. The poem ends with both Athena and Zeus causing a cessation of hostilities between the family of Odysseus and the various clan members of the slain suitors, and so the conditions of vendetta or *lex talionis* in the plot and narrative are closed.[25]

As we noted earlier, there is a putative seventh period of narration that is brief, summary and retrospective, beginning at Scroll Twenty-Three, line 310. In this synopsis of his travels there is no mention of the antagonism of Poseidon or of the constant collaborative agency of the deity Athena. This retrospect is given in the voice of King Odysseus and is addressed to his queen and the mother of his son, as husband and wife lie abed together, at last intimately and politically united and before they fall asleep; the consciousness of

23 The seventeenth-century composer Monteverdi, with his opera *Il Ritorno d'Ulisse in Patria*, slightly changed the final recognition scene which takes place between husband and wife; in the *libretto* by Badoaro the hero is able to describe the design and patterning of his queen's bedlinen to her, thus proving his intimacy and identity. They then sing a duet, 'My sun long sighed for, my light renewed'. See Rosand and Vartolo, 2007.

24 There is an indication of the contempt which Achilles holds for Odysseus in the Homeric Iliad, IX,308, and, of course, we have seen how in the first song of Demodocus there is another moment of profound contention occurring between these two heroes who both appear in each other's poem where they unambiguously oppose each other. The worlds or poetry of Odysseus and Achilles are immiscible, and when Odysseus portrays Achilles in Scroll Eleven, mimicking his speech in Hades, Achilles is caused to appear as thoroughly diminished and abjected.

25 As we observed earlier in Chapter 3, the legal qualities of the Homeric Iliad are likewise founded upon a complex system of *mutual vengeance*, where *ápoina*, 'ransom', and *poinē*, 'blood price', are exchanged. The initial statements of this moral economy are represented by the movement of women and the reciprocal offering of movable wealth: these women being Helen, Chryseis and Briseis. Patroclus and Hector are likewise essential to this metaphor of exchange or what is in fact a metonymy of violence.

this nuclear family has been integrated and has been in fact *sealed* by an act of terrific and retributive bloodshed.[26]

There is, finally, the overall poem writ large, the Homeric Odyssey, which can be construed as the eighth and complete order of narrative, insofar as it contains all the previous seven periodic perspectives of the song in their complicated and interstitial coherence.

It is appropriate that the Muse, Zeus and Athena all mention how the anger of Poseidon delays and causes deviation in the return of Odysseus and in Scroll Two the poets – given in the voice of the Muse – mention those awful events which occurred with the Cyclops, the son of Poseidon, an occasion when the protocols of hospitality were doubly violated.[27] To repeat the above point, the hero himself, in his account of his voyage in Scrolls Nine to Twelve, makes reference to the cause of Poseidon's wrath, but in his retrospective summary of the whole voyage in Scroll Twenty-Three, lines 310–43, he ignores the agency of this deity, just as he does not mention the overruling and determinative influence of Athena on his travels.

It is noteworthy that in Scroll Thirteen of the Homeric Iliad Poseidon is a deity who assumes several differing identities and speaks with different voices; that is, he is profoundly polytropic and personably various and fully mimetic of other subjects.[28] Like Odysseus, he is a figure whose consciousness and voice are able to change at will.

There are thus three levels or internal cycles in the epic narrative of king-hero Odysseus. There is the basic plot as evinced by the dialogues of Zeus and Athena; there is the *hearsay* which tells of the hero's actions in varying times and places; and there is the individual story extolled by Odysseus himself in Scrolls Nine to Twelve and in micronarrative form in Scroll Twenty-Three. One might argue that these three dimensions concern the supernal and divine perspective, the mortal world of 'hearsay' and the heroic self-aggrandizing

26 At this point all the narrative periods have converged and met: *Le Temps Retrouvé*, as it were.

27 In Scroll Two there is another instance where the proto-poet or outer poet says something which is only otherwise mentioned by Odysseus in his song to the Phaeacian court; this is a reference to the Cyclops at ii,19. Again, we observe the symmetry between outer poet and 'inner' Odysseus. Also in Scroll Two there is what must be the unique occasion where a deity invokes another deity and delivers a speech act: this occurs where Athena in the guise of Mentor prays to Poseidon (iii,55–61). Athena is here present at a formal and magnificent sacrificial rite which Nestor is offering at the feast of Poseidon. Let us recall that Nestor is the grandson of Poseidon through Neleus (xi,254).

28 Proteus is another figure – like Poseidon, Athena and Odysseus – who is polymorphic. He, almost like a narrator himself, is aware of the trials and travails of Odysseus, including his long sojourn with Calypso (iv,383–569).

personal narrative which is expressed by the returning warrior himself. The latter two narrations tend towards story rather than plot.

Somewhat like Vyāsa, Athena is both a generator of the poem and a constant agent within its working. As an actual voice, she appears in the fourth place, after the first words of the poet, after the Muse has begun to sing and after Zeus offers the first dramatically expressed words of the poem: poet > Muse > Zeus > Athena – this is the sequence. She is the primary character to physically name 'Odysseus'. As we have noted, she too is polymorphic and is able to change her form, appearance and voice and appear in the persona of numerous and diverse characters; she too is a master of fiction.

The final words of the poem mention this labile quality and how it was Mentor, the companion of Odysseus, whom she was really most *like*. Pertinently, it was the mortal and human Mentor to whom Odysseus had entrusted the care of his palace and kingdom when he departed for Troy (ii,225–26). This figure of Mentor is the one whom the poets say that Athena is most comparable to, and so again, the audience perceive another dimension to the pliable and malleable deity and her uniquely narrative force, as well as another aspect of kinship or amity between the divine and mortally heroic. Odysseus chose well when he selected Mentor to be his guardian agent or domestic factotum.

In Scroll Twenty-Four, Zeus comments that it was Athena who devised the plot of the poem, that is, the narrative of Odysseus when he had returned to the isle of Ithaca (xxiv,487–82). He had also said this earlier, at v,22–24. Certainly, Athena is constantly directing Telemachus, Penelope and Odysseus as the poem progresses, and – as we know – she does at times literally originate the plot. In this I would argue that divine Athena is akin to the *ṛṣi* Vyāsa in that they both initially generate and then participate in and manage events of the plot which, in the case of Homeric Odyssey, presents to an audience, and nowadays to a modern reader, the organized and integrated consciousness of *diogenès oduseùs*, 'divine Odysseus'. Without her presence and direction there is only story.

ACHILLES

As a short supplement to the above, let us offer a cursory outline of the narrative form of the Homeric Iliad, a poem which is far more linear in movement than the song of Odysseus.[29] The epic opens by beginning with an indefinite moment in the past, and then the narrative moves forward until it reaches the textual present 9 days later at I,53. Then there is another pause of

29 The summary of the epic of heroic Rāma, as given in Book Five of the *Great Bhārata*, V,258–76, similarly partakes of a generally singular and unified narrative.

12 days before Thetis visits Zeus and the *will of Zeus* – derived from a speech act of Thetis, itself partially derived from a speech act of her son Achilles – takes effect and establishes the plot; Zeus himself reiterates the core of this at XV,52–77.[30]

The first day of battle then continues from the beginning of Scroll Two until halfway through Scroll Seven. Thus, serial time is amplified and compressed by the poets and is not given in a simple uniform sequence of hours and days. The next day, the second day of fighting, in terms of poetry only lasts from VII,433–82. Scroll Eight is one day in itself, the third, and Scroll Nine is the evening and night of that day, a darkness which extends into Scroll Ten and the ambush scene where Odysseus and Diomedes cross the lines of battle. Scroll Eleven begins the great fourth day when the Trojans reach the beached Greek fleet, and this time continues until Scroll Sixteen when Patroclus is felled and the warriors struggle over his corpse. His death marks the conclusion of general combat.

Thereafter follows a period which concerns Achilles and his grief for Patroclus and his vengeance upon Hector. Scroll Nineteen commences with the fifth day, where the mourning and despair of Achilles are delineated; this day continues with certain deities themselves participating in the contention of warriors in Scroll Twenty and Twenty-One and with Achilles returning to the combat. Once Hector has been slain in Scroll Twenty-Two, the fifth day closes and Achilles at last sleeps again. On the sixth day, lamentation is performed by the Greeks and the obsequies for Patroclus are accomplished. On the seventh day the funeral games are performed, and on the eighth Thetis and Zeus again confer, for the will of Zeus as committed in Scroll One has now come to term and the central and master narrative – the plot – of the epic begins to close. On the night of that day Priam visits Achilles and claims the body of Hector, and then follow eleven days before his funeral rites are accomplished; there the poem concludes with the implication of a renewal of warfare.

Different heroes receive varying focus from the poets at different moments in this formal narrative: Achilles, Diomedes, Odysseus, Hector, Aias, Patroclus and others receive the narrative concentration as the aim of the poem pauses for a while, favouring the character and deeds of a particular hero until it moves towards another figure in the drama. This is part of the narrative form, this shifting of attention and visual focus that individually highlights a warrior's *aristeía* or 'valour'.

---

30 It can be argued that – with the speech act of Thetis, itself founded upon Achilles's own words and then given force by Zeus himself – Achilles, until Scroll XVIII, is staging his own epic and makes his own *kléos*.

There are also timeless interludes in the narration, as when the world and lives of the deities are being described as if in changeless capsules which run parallel to the earthly and temporal world. Such a moment, for instance, also occurs in Scroll Eighteen when the poets portray the divine Shield whose imagery lacks all timely transition and is similarly undecaying and immortal. Thus this Iliadic narration is extremely different from and *unlike* what occurs in the Homeric Odyssey, which, for its irrational complexity, is much more akin in form to what we as readers today can perceive in the multitudinous narrative dimensions, perspectives and sequences of the *Great Bhārata*.

There is one irrational element in the Homeric Iliad and that concerns how Thetis and Zeus both repeatedly announce that the death of young Achilles is imminent. No reason underlines this fact, and it is as if the demise of Achilles is a *null point* in the poem, a hypothetical instant which does not occur and yet which drives the movement of the narrative forward, for this comprehension which Achilles receives from his mother informs and influences all events in the poem, insofar as the narrative is activated by the speech act of Achilles to Thetis in Scroll One, which is then conveyed to Zeus and cosmically affirmed.

As we have seen, this becomes the plot of the poem, and the knowledge of the youthful hero's impending demise is something which actually precedes all narrative exposition and is rationally inexplicable: it has no metonymical or causal origin. Both the death of Achilles and that of Odysseus are predicted throughout their respective poems yet neither occasion occurs within those songs, for both epics cleverly evade perfect closure. In a way this is akin to how the hypothetical *ur*-poem of Vyāsa supplies the motive zero which facilitates the generation of the plot.

What is remarkable is how similar in fundamental narrative structure are the Homeric Odyssey and Iliad: in terms of the primary nature of the narrative generated by a speech act of Zeus in company with a feminine deity, and in terms of the time lapsed in both poems. The editors of these two works obviously prepared their texts with a similar template in mind.[31]

31 For the concerned reader, I would urge them to see McGrath, 2016, pp. 179–89, 'Appendix on Epic Achilles'.

BIBLIOGRAPHY

Agrawal, Ashvini. 1989. *Rise and Fall of the Imperial Guptas*. Motilal Banarsidass, Delhi.

Agrawal, D. P. 1971. *The Copper Bronze Age in India*. Munshiram Manoharlal, New Delhi.

———. 2007. *The Indus Civilisation*. Aryan Books International, New Delhi.

Agrawala, P. K. 1965. 'The Depiction of Punch-Marked Coins in Early Indian Art'. *Journal of the Numismatic Society of India* 27, pp. 170–76.

Agrawala, Vasudeva S. 1952. *India as Known to Pāṇini*. Prithvi Kumar, Varanasi.

Allchin, F. R. 1995. *The Archaeology of Early Historic South Asia*. Cambridge University Press, Cambridge.

Allen, N. J. 1996. 'The Hero's Five Relations: A Proto Indo-European Story'. In J. Leslie (ed.), *Myth and Mythmaking: Continuous Evolution in Indian Tradition*, pp. 5–20. Curzon, London.

———. 1999. 'Arjuna and the Second Function: A Dumézilian Crux'. *Journal of the Royal Asiatic Society*, Third Series, 9(3), November, pp. 403–18.

Andrijanic, Ivan, and Sven Sellmer (eds). 2016. *On the Growth and Composition of the Sanskrit Epics and Puranas: Proceedings of the Fifth Dubrovnik International Conference on the Sanskrit Epics and Puranas*. Croatian Academy of Sciences and Arts, Ibis Grafika, Zagreb.

Anthony, David W. 2007. *The Horse, the Wheel, and Language*. Princeton University Press, Princeton, NJ.

Aristotle. 1953. *Poetics*. Edited by W. Hamilton Fyfe. Loeb Classics, Cambridge, MA.

Austin, J. L. 1962. *How to Do Things with Words*. Harvard University Press, Cambridge, MA.

Bachvarova, M. R. 2016. *From Hittite to Homer*. Cambridge University Press, Cambridge.

Bakker, E. 1997. *Poetry in Speech*. Cornell University Press, Ithaca, NY.

———. 2005. *Pointing at the Past*. Center for Hellenic Studies, Washington, DC.

Bandyopadhyay, Sibaji, 2016. *Three Essays on the Mahābhārata*. Orient Black Swan, New Delhi.

Barber, E. J. W. 1991. *Prehistoric Textiles*. Princeton University Press, Princeton, NJ.

Bean, Susan S., and Shashi Tharoor. 2006. *Epic India. M.F. Husain's Mahabharata Project*, Salem, MA.

Bedekar, V. M. 1963. 'Dhyānayoga in the Mahābhārata'. *Bhāratīya Vidya* 20–21, pp. 116–25.Benveniste, Emile. 1969. *Le Vocabulaire des Institutions Indo-européennes*. Two vols. Les Editions de Minuit, Paris. Republished 2016, *Dictionary of Indo-European Concepts and Society*, trans. E. Palmer. HAU Books, Chicago, IL.

Bergren, Ann. 2008. *Weaving Truth*. Hellenic Studies Series, 19. Harvard University Press, Cambridge, MA.

Bhartṛthari. 2015. *Vākpadīyam*. Caukhambā Saṃskṛta Sīrīja Āphisa, Varanasi, India.

Bhattacharya, Pradip. 2009. The Mahabharata in Arabic and Persian. Available at: http://www.boloji.com/articles/752/the-mahabharata-in-arabic-and-persian (accessed 13 May 2019).

Blackburn, Simon. 2018. *On Truth.* Oxford University Press, New York.

Blackburn, Stuart H., et al. (eds). 1989. *Oral Epics in India.* University of California Press, Berkeley.

Bose, Sugata. 2017. *The Nation as Mother and Other Visions of Nationhood.* Penguin Books, New Delhi.

Bottino, A. P. 2014. 'The Trees of Laertes'. Available at: https://chs.harvard.edu/CHS/article/display/1304 (accessed 13 May 2019).

———. 2015. 'The Pharos of Laertes'. Available at: https://chs.harvard.edu/CHS/article/display/1304 (accessed 13 May 2019).

———. 2016. 'The Adverb ΑΝΔΡΑΚΑΣ and the Composition of the Odyssey'. Available at: https://chs.harvard.edu/CHS/article/display/1304 (accessed 13 May 2019).

———. 2017. 'Space, Time, and Remembering in the Orchard of Laertes'. Available at: https://chs.harvard.edu/CHS/article/display/1304 (accessed 13 May 2019).

Bowles, Adam. 2007. *Dharma, Disorder, and the Political in Ancient India.* Brill, Leiden.

Brereton, Joel. 2009. 'Dhárman in the Ṛgveda'. In P. Olivelle (ed.), *Dharma: Studies in Its Semantic, Cultural, and Religious History*, pp. 27–67. Motilal Banarsidass, New Delhi.

Brockington, John. 2003. 'Yoga in the Mahābhārata'. In I. Whicher and D. Carpenter (eds), *Yoga: The Indian Tradition*, pp. 13–24. Routledge Curzon, London.

Brockington, John, and Mary Brockington. 2006. *Rāma the Steadfast.* Penguin Books, London.

Bronkhorst, Johannes. 1993. *The Two Sources of Indian Asceticism.* P. Lang, Bern.

———. 2007. *Greater Magadha.* Brill, Leiden.

———. 2011a. *Buddhism in the Shadow of Brahmanism.* Brill, Leiden.

———. 2011b. *Karma.* University of Hawai'i Press, Honolulu.

———. 2011c. *Language and Reality.* Brill, Leiden.

Bronkhorst, Johannes, and Madhav M. Despande. 1999. *Aryan and Non-Aryan in South Asia.* Harvard Oriental Series, Opera Minora Vol. 3. Harvard University Press, Cambridge, MA.

Brown, Cecil Jermyn. 1922. *The Coins of India.* Association Press, Calcutta.

Brown, W. Norman. 1972. 'Duty as Truth in Ancient India'. *Proceedings of the American Philosophical Society* 116, pp. 252–68.

Bruckner, Heidrun, Hugh van Skyhawk and Claus Peter Zollner (eds). 2007. *The Concept of the Hero in Indian Culture.* Manohar, New Delhi.

Bruner, J. 1991. 'The Narrative Construction of Reality'. *Critical Inquiry* 18, pp. 1–21.

Bühler, G. 1886. *The Laws of Manu.* Oxford Clarendon Press, Oxford.

Burgess, Jonathan S. 2001. *The Tradition of the Trojan War in Homer and the Epic Cycle.* Johns Hopkins University Press, Baltimore, MD.

Burkert, Walter. 1987. 'The Making of Homer in the Sixth Century BC: Rhapsodes Versus Stesichorus'. In *Papers on the Amasis Painter and His World*, pp. 43–62. Getty Museum, Malibu.

Bynum, David E. 1974. *Four Generations of Oral Literary Studies at Harvard University.* Center for the Study of Oral Literature, Harvard University, Cambridge, MA.

Coningham, Robin, and Ruth Young. 2015. *The Archaeology of South Asia.* Cambridge University Press, New York.

Corballis, Michael C. 2017. *The Truth about Language.* University of Chicago Press, Chicago, IL.

Couture, Andre. 2015. *Kṛṣṇa in the Harivaṅśa.* D. K. Printworld, New Delhi.

Dandekar, R. N. 1990. *The Mahābhārata Revisited.* Sahitya Akademi, New Delhi.

Das, Gurcharan. 2009. *The Difficulty of Being Good*. Allen Lane, Delhi.

Davidson, O. M. 1998. 'The Text of Ferdowsī's *Shāhnāma* and the Burden of the Past'. *Journal of the American Oriental Society* 118, pp. 63–68.

———. 2013. *Poet and Hero in the Persian Book of Kings*. 3rd ed. Ilex Foundation, Boston, MA; Harvard University Press, Cambridge, MA.

Davies, Malcolm. 2016. *The Aithiopis*. Harvard University Press, Cambridge, MA.

Deshpande, C. R. 1978. *The Transmission of the Mahābhārata Tradition*. Indian Institute of Advanced Studies, Simla.

Dickey, Eleanor. 2007. *Ancient Greek Scholarship*. Oxford University Press, Oxford.

Diodorus of Sicily. 1939. *Library of History*. C. H. Oldfather (ed. and trans.), 12 vols. Loeb Editions, Harvard University Press, Cambridge MA.

Dodd, Nigel. 2014. *The Social Life of Money*. Princeton University Press, Princeton, NJ.

Donald, Merlin. 1991. *Origins of the Modern Mind*. Harvard University Press, Cambridge, MA.

Doris, John M. 2002. *Lack of Character*. Cambridge University Press, New York.

Doshi, Saryu. 1982. 'Paliyas of Saurasthra'. In S. Settar and G.-D. Sontheimer (eds), *Memorial Stones: A Study of Their Origin, Significance and Variety*, pp. 157–73. Institute of Indian Art, New Delhi.

Dué, Casey. 2019. *Achilles Unbound*. Hellenic Studies Series, 81. Center for Hellenic Studies, Washington, DC.

Dumézil, Georges. 1940. *Mitra-Varuna*. Leroux, Presses Universitaires de France. 1948, Editions Gallimard, Paris, reprint.

———. 1968. *Mythe et Épopée*. Vol. 1. Gallimard, Paris.

———. 1977. *Les Dieux Souverains des Indo-Européens*. Gallimard, Paris.

Dumont, Louis. 1966. *Homo Hierarchicus*. Editions Gallimard, Paris.

Eck, Diana L. 1981. *Darśan: Seeing the Divine in India*. Anima Books, Chambersburg.

———. 2012. *India: A Sacred Geography*. Harmony Books, New York.

Egginton, William. 2016. *The Man Who Invented Fiction*. Bloomsbury, New York.

Elgood, Robert. 2017. *Rajput Arms and Armour*, 2 vols. Niyogi Books, Delhi.

Elmer, David. 2013. *The Poetics of Consent*. Johns Hopkins University Press, Baltimore, MD.

Evans-Pritchard, E. E. 1940. *The Nuer*. Oxford University Press, Oxford.

Farnell, L. R. 1921. *Greek Hero Cults and Ideas of Immortality*. Clarendon Press, Oxford.

Feller, Danielle. 2012. 'Epic Heroes Have No Childhood'. *Indologica Taurinensia* 38, pp. 65–85.

Figgis, Mike. 2017. *The 36 Dramatic Situations*. Faber and Faber, London.

Finlay, Stephen. 2014. *A Confusion of Tongues*. Oxford University Press, New York.

Finley, Moses I. 1954. *The World of Odysseus*. Viking Press, New York.

———. 1973. *The Ancient Economy*. University of California Press, Berkeley.

Fitzgerald, James. 2001. 'Making Yudhiṣṭhira the King: The Dialectics and Politics of Violence in the *Mahābhārata*'. *Rocznik Orientalistczny* 54, pp. 63–92.

———. 2006. 'Negotiating the Shape of "Scripture"'. In P. Olivelle (ed.), *Between the Empires*, pp. 257–86. Oxford University Press, New York.

Flueckiger, Joyce Burkhalter. 1996. *Gender and Genre in the Folklore of Middle India*. Cornell University Press, Ithaca, NY.

Fortson, Benjamin W. 2004. *Indo-European Language and Culture*. Blackwell, Oxford. Second edition, 2010.

Frame, Douglas. 2009. *Hippota Nestor*. Center for Hellenic Studies, Washington, DC.

Frasca, Richard. 1984. *The Theatre of the Mahābhārata*. University of Hawaii Press, Honolulu.

Friedrich, P. 1966. 'Proto-Indo-European Kinship'. In *Ethnology* 5(1), pp. 1–36.

Gandhi, M. K. 1927. *Autobiography: My Experiments with Truth*. Navajivan Publishing House, Ahmedabad.

Gerety, Finnian M. M. 2015. 'This Whole World Is OM: Song, Soteriology, and the Emergence of the Sacred Syllable'. PhD dissertation, Harvard University Archives.

———. 2018. 'Digital Guru: Embodiment, Technology, and the Transmission of Traditional Knowledge in Kerala'. In *Asian Ethnology* 77(1–2), pp. 3–31.

Ghurye, G. S. 1972. *Two Brahminical Institutions, Gotra and Charana*. Popular Prakashan, Bombay.

Gitomer, David L. 1992. 'King Duryodhana: The Mahābhārata Discourse of King and Virtue in Epic and Drama'. *Journal of the American Oriental Society* 112(2), pp. 222–32.

Goldman, Robert P. 1977. *Gods, Priests, and Warriors: The Bhṛgus of the Mahābhārata*. Columbus University Press, New York.

———. 2015. 'Poet as Seer, Poetry as Seen'. In G. Thompson (ed.), *Beyond Rules: Essays Honoring the Life and Work of Frtiz Staal*, pp. 1–26. Honolulu International Journal of Buddhist Studies.

Graeber, David. 2001. *Towards an Anthropological Theory of Value*. Palgrave, New York.

Graeber, David, and Marshall Sahlins. 2017. *On Kingship*. HAU Books, Chicago, IL.

Graziosi, Barbara. 2002. *Inventing Homer: The Early Reception of Epic*. Cambridge University Press, Cambridge.

Hardy, Thomas. 1904. *The Dynasts*. Macmillan, New York.

Hegarty, James. 2012. *Religion, Narrative and Public Imagination in South Asia: Past and Place in the Sanskrit Mahābhārata*. Routledge, London.

Hellwig, Oliver. 2009. 'Etymological Trends in Sanskrit Vocabulary'. *Digital Scholarship in the Humanities* 25(1), pp. 105–18. Available at: https://doi.org/10.1093/llc/fqp034 (accessed 13 May 2019).

———. 2017. 'Stratifying the Mahābhārata'. *Indo-Iranian Journal* 60(2), pp. 132–69.

Herodotus. 1918. *Histories*. Translated by A. T. Murray, 4 vols. Loeb Classical Library, Cambridge, MA.

Herzfeld, Michael. 1985. *The Poetics of Manhood*. Princeton University Press, Princeton, NJ.

Hesiod. 1914. *Theogony and Works & Days*. Edited by H. G. Evelyn-White. Loeb Classical Library, Cambridge, MA.

Hiltebeitel, A. 1979. 'Kṛṣṇa and the Mahābhārata'. *Annals of the Bhandarkar Oriental Research Institute* 60, pp. 65–107.

———. 1982. 'Brothers, Friends, and Charioteers: Parallel Episodes in the Irish and Indian Epics'. In E. Polomé (ed.), *Homage to Georges Dumézil, Journal of Indo-European Studies* 3, pp. 85–111.

———. 1988, 1991. *The Cult of Draupadī*, 2 vols. University of Chicago Press, Chicago, IL.

———. 1999. *Rethinking India's Oral and Classical Epics*. University of Chicago Press, Chicago, IL.

———. 2006. 'Aśvaghoṣa's Buddhacarita'. *Journal of Indian Philosophy* 34, pp. 229–86.

———. 2010. *Dharma*. University of Hawai'i Press, Honolulu.

———. 2011a. 'On Sukthankar's "S" and Some Shortsighted Assessments and Uses of the Pune Critical Edition'. *Journal of Vaiṣṇava Studies* 19(2), pp. 87–126.

———. 2011b. *Reading the Fifth Veda*. Brill, Leiden.

———. 2011c. *Dharma: Its Early History in Law, Religion, and Narrative*. Oxford University Press, New York.

———. 2018a. *Freud's India*. Oxford University Press, New York.

———. 2018b. *Freud's Mahābhārata*. Oxford University Press, New York.

Hitch, Sarah. 2009. *King of Sacrifice*. Center for Hellenic Studies, Harvard University Press, Cambridge, MA.
Holtzmann, Adolf. 1879. *Arjuna*. Trübner, Strassburg.
———. 1892. *Zur Geschichte und Kritik des Mahābhārata*. C. F. Haeseler, Kiel.
Homer. [1919] 2002. *Odyssey*. Translated by A. T. Murray and revised by George E. Dimock. 2 vols. Loeb Editions, Harvard University Press, Cambridge MA.
———. [1924] 2003. *Iliad*. Translated by A. T. Murray and revised by William F. Wyatt. 2 vols. Loeb Editions, Harvard University Press, Cambridge MA.
Hopkins, E. Washburn. 1888. 'The Social and Military Position of the Ruling Caste in Ancient India'. *Journal of the American Oriental Society* 13, pp. 57–372.
———. 1894. 'Henotheism in the Rig-Veda'. In *Classical Studies in Honour of Henry Drisler*, pp. 75–83. Macmillan, London.
———. 1901a. 'Yoga Technique in the Great Epic'. *Journal of the American Oriental Society* 22, pp. 333–79.
———. 1901b. *The Great Epic of India*. Scribner and Sons, New York. Repr., Motilal Banarsidass, Delhi, 1993.
———. 1907. 'The Sniff-Kiss in Ancient India'. *Journal of the American Oriental Society*, 28, pp. 120–34.
———. 1915. *Epic Mythology*. Trübner, Strasburg.
———. 1931. 'The Divinity of Kings'. *Journal of the American Oriental Society* 51, pp. 309–16.
Hornell, James. 1942. 'Hero-Memorial Stones of Kathiawar'. *Antiquity* 16(64), pp. 289–300.
Jacobsen, Knut A. (ed.). 2012. *Yoga Power*. Brill, Leiden.
Jakobson, Roman. 1981. *Essais de Linguistique Générale*. Les Editions de Minuit, Paris.
———. 1987. *Language in Literature*. Krystyna Pomorska and Stephen Rudy (eds). Harvard University Press, Cambridge, MA.
Jamison, Stephanie. 1994. 'Draupadi on the Walls of Troy'. *Classical Antiquity* 13(1), April, pp. 5–16.
———. 1996. *Sacrificed Wife/Sacrificer's Wife*. Oxford University Press, New York.
———. 1997. 'A Gāndharva Marriage in the Odyssey'. In *Studies in Honour of Jaan Puhvel*, Part II. *Journal of Indo-European Studies*, monograph 21.
———. 2007. *The Rig Veda between Two Worlds*. Collège de France, Publications de l'Institut de Civilisation Indienne, Série in 8, Fascicule 74. Editions Diffusion de Broccard, Paris.
Jamison, Stephanie, and Joel Brereton. 2014. *The Rigveda: The Earliest Religious Poetry of India*. 2 vols. Oxford University Press, New York
Jhala, Angma Dey. 2008. *Courtly Indian Women in Late Imperial India*. Pickering and Chatto, London.
———. 2011. *Royal Patronage, Power and Aesthetics in Princely India*. Pickering and Chatto, London.
——— (ed.). 2018. *The Peacock in the Desert*. Yale University Press, New Haven, CT.
Jhala, Jayasinhji. 1991. 'Marriage, Hierarchy, and Identity in Ideology and Practice'. PhD dissertation, Harvard University Archives.
de Jong, Irene J. F. 2001. *A Narratological Commentary on the Odyssey*. Cambridge University Press, New York.
de Jong, Irene J. F., René Nünlist and Angus Bowie. 2004. *Narrators, Narratees, and Narratives in Ancient Greek Literature*. Brill, Leiden.
Kalhoro, Zulfiqar Ali. 2009. 'Tombs of Fallen Heroes'. *Suomen Anthropologi* 34(3), pp. 44–55.
———. 2010. 'Vanishing Visual Heritage: Sati and Hero-Stones in Nagarparkar, Sindh'. *Journal of Indian Society of Oriental Art* 27, pp. 231–38.

———. 2014. 'Representations of the Romance of Suhni-Mehar in the Kalhora Tombs (1680–1783), Sindh, Pakistan'. *Journal of Asian Civilizations* 37(1), July, pp. 27–45.

———. 2015. 'One Deity, Three Temples: A Typology of Sacred of Spaces in Hariyar Village, Tharparkar Sindh'. *Research Deliberation* 1(2), November, pp. 19–35.

———. 2017. *Memorial Stones of Tharparkar.* EFT: Endowment Fund Trust for Preservation of the Heritage of Sindh, Karachi.

Keith, Arthur Berriedale. 1908. 'The Battle between the Pāṇḍavas and Kauravas'. *Journal of the Royal Asiatic Society* 40(3), July, pp. 831–36.

Kerrigan, John. 2018. *Shakespeare's Originality*. Oxford University Press, Oxford.

Klostermaier, Klaus K. 1984. *Mythologies and Philosophies of Salvation in the Theistic Traditions of India.* Canadian Corporation for Studies in Religion, Ontario.

Kohl, Philip L. 2007. *The Making of Bronze Age Eurasia.* Cambridge University Press, Cambridge.

Kölver, Bernhard. 1997. *Staat und Recht im Klassischen Indien.* Oldenbourg, Munchen.

Konstan, David, and Kurt A. Raaflaub (eds). 2010. *Epic and History.* Wiley Blackwell, Chichester.

Koskikallio, Petteri (ed). 2009. *Parallels and Comparisons: Proceedings of the Fourth Dubrovnik International Conference on the Sanskrit Epics and Puranas.* Croatian Academy of Sciences and Arts, Ibis Grafika, Zagreb.

Kumar, Girja. 2016, 2017. *The Mahabharatans.* 2 vols. Har-Anand Publications, New Delhi.

Laine, J. W. 1989. *Visions of God: Narratives of Theophany in the Mahābhārata.* Institute for Indology, Vienna.

Lakoff, G., and M. Johnson. *Metaphors We Live By.* University of Chicago Press, Chicago, IL.

Lévi-Strausse, Claude. 1962. *La Pensée Sauvage.* Librairie Plon, Paris.

Lienhardt, Godfrey. 1961. *Divinity and Experience.* Clarendon Press, Oxford.

Loizeau, Rachel. 2015–16. 'Indian Epics in Khmer Art'. *Marg* 67(2), pp. 32–47.

Lord, A. B. 1960. *The Singer of Tales.* Harvard University Press, Cambridge, MA.

Lubotsky, Alexander. 1996. 'The Iconography of the Vishnu Temple at Deogarh'. *Ars Orientalis* 26, pp. 65–80.

Maas, Philip. 2016. 'On the Meaning of jhāna and dhyāna "Meditation" in Early Buddhism, the Mokṣadharmaparvan of the Mahābhārata, and in Classical Yoga Philosophy'. Available at: https://www.academia.edu/30127734/On_the_Meaning_of_jhāna_and_dhyāna_Meditation_in_Early_Buddhism_the_Mokṣadharmaparvan_of_the_Mahābhārata_and_in_Classical_Yoga_ Philosophy (accessed 13 May 2019).

MacMurdo, James. 1820. 'An Account of the Province of Cutch'. In *Transactions of the Literary Society of Bombay* 2, pp. 205–41.

Mahābhārata. 1933–66. 19 vols. BORI, Poona.

Mahābhāratam, with commentary of Nīlakaṇṭha, edited by Pandit Kinjawadekar. 1979. 6 vols. Oriental Books Reprint Corporation, New Delhi.

Mahadevan, T. P. 2008. 'On the Southern Recension of the Mahābhārata, Brahman Migrations, and the Brāhmī Paleography'. *Electronic Journal of Vedic Studies* 15(2), pp. 43–147.

———. 2011. 'Three Rails of the Mahābhārata Text Tradition'. *Journal of Vaiṣṇava Studies* 19(2), pp. 23–69.

Malafouris, Lambros. 2008. 'Between Brains, Bodies and Things'. *Philosophical Transactions of the Royal Society* B 363, pp. 1993–2002. Available at: doi:10.1098/rstb.2008.0014 (accessed 13 May 2019).

Malinar, A. 2012a. 'Duryodhana's Truths: Kingship and Divinity in *Mahābhārata* 5.60'. In J. Brockington (ed.), *Battle, Bards and Brāhmins*, pp. 51–78. Motilal Banarsidass, Delhi.

———. 2012b. 'Yoga Power in the Mahābhārata'. In K. A. Jacobsen (ed.), *Yoga Power*, pp. 33–60. Brill, Leiden.

Malinowski, Bronislaw. 1923. 'The Problem of Meaning in Primitive Languages'. In C. K. Ogden and I. A. Richards (eds), *The Meaning of Meaning*, pp. 296–336. Kegan Paul, Trench and Trubner, London.

Mallinson, James, and Mark Singleton. 2017. *Roots of Yoga*. Penguin Books, London.

Mallory, J. P., and Douglas Q. Adams. 1997. *Encyclopedia of Indo-European Culture*. Fitzroy Dearborn, London.

Mani, Vettam. 1964. *A Purāṇic Encyclopaedia*. Repr., Motilal Banarsidass, Delhi, 1975.

Mankekar, Purnima. 1999. *Screening Culture*. Duke University Press, Durham, NC.

Manusmṛti. 1983. With Sanskrit commentary from Manvartha-Muktāvalī of Kullūka Bhaṭṭa. Motilal Banarsidass, Delhi.

Martin, Richard P. 1989. *The Language of Heroes*. Cornell University Press, Ithaca, NY.

———. 2018. *Mythologizing Performance*. Cornell University Press, Ithaca, NY.

Mason, Daniel Philippe. 2017. 'The Rack of His Imagination'. *Academic Psychiatry* 41, pp. 1–4. 10.1007/s40596-017-0807-0.

Mauss, Marcel, and Henri Hubert. 1902–4. 'Esquisse d'une Théorie Générale de la Magie'. *Année Sociologique* 7, pp. 1–146.

———. 1925. *Essai sur le Don*. Alcan, Paris.

McGrath, Kevin. 2000. Review of Wendy Doniger, 'Splitting the Difference'. *American Anthropologist* 102(2), p. 417.

———. 2003. 'The Swim as a Work of Art'. *Keats-Shelley Review* 17, pp. 114–19.

———. 2004a. *The Sanskrit Hero: Karṇa in Epic Mahābhārata*. Brill, Leiden.

———. 2004b. 'Walking in the Morea'. *Temenos Academy Review* 6, pp. 88–116.

———. 2009. *Strī: Women in Epic Mahābhārata*. Ilex Foundation, Harvard University Press. Repr., Orient Black Swan, New Delhi, 2011.

———. 2011. *Jaya: Performance in Epic Mahābhārata*. Ilex Foundation, Harvard University Press, Cambridge, MA.

———. 2012a. 'A Short Note on Arjuna as a Semi-Divine Being'. *Journal of Vaiṣṇava Studies* 21(1), Fall issue, pp. 199–210.

———. 2012b. 'Heroic Kṛṣṇa: Portrait of a Charioteer'. In Festschrift for Gregory Nagy: *Donum natalicium digitaliter confectum Gregorio Nagy septuagenario a discipulis collegis familiaribus oblatum*. Available at: https://chs.harvard.edu/CHS/article/display/4359 (accessed 13 May 2019).

———. 2013. *Heroic Kṛṣṇa: Friendship in Epic Mahābhārata*. Ilex Foundation, Harvard University Press, Cambridge, MA.

———. 2014. 'Acts and Conditions of the Gītā'. In S. Tsoukalas and G. Surya (eds), *Studies in the Bhagavad Gita: Ontology*, pp. 43–92. Edwin Mellen Press, Lewiston, NY.

———. 2015a. *In the Kacch*. McFarland, Jefferson, NC.

———. 2015b. 'Walking in the Banni'. *Temenos Academy Review* 18, pp. 129–45.

———. 2016. *Arjuna Pāṇḍava: The Double Hero in Epic Mahābhārata*. Orient Black Swan, New Delhi.

———. 2017a. *Rāja Yudhiṣṭhira: Kingship in Epic Mahābhārata*. Cornell University Press, Ithaca, NY; Orient Black Swan, New Delhi.

———. 2017b. 'Kingship, Landscape, and the Hero'. In J. Jhala (ed.), *Genealogy, Archive, Image*, chapter 4, pp. 83–120. De Gruyter Open, Warsaw.

———. 2018a. 'Bhīṣma Devavrata and Āhiṃsa'. *Journal of Vaiṣṇava Studies* 26(2), Spring, pp. 77–86.

———. 2018b. *Bhīṣma Devavrata: Authority in Epic Mahābhārata*. Anthem Press, New Delhi.

———. 2018c. 'Art of Travel'. *Harvard Review* 52, pp. 11–22.

———. 2019. 'Homeric Iliad and Epic Mahābhārata'. In K. Roy and N. Dayal (eds), *Questioning Paradigms, Constucting Histories: A Festschrift for Romila Thapar*, pp. 312–26. Aleph Book Company, New Delhi.

McHugh, James Andrew. 2012. *Sandalwood and Carrion: Smell in Indian Religion and Culture.* Oxford University Press, New York.

Michaels, Axel (ed.). 2001. *The Pandit: Traditional Scholarship in India.* Manohar, Delhi.

Minchin, Elizabeth. 2001. *Homer and the Resources of Memory*. Oxford University Press, New York.

Minkowski, Christopher Z. 1992. *Priesthood in Ancient India: A Study of the Maitrāvaruṇa Priest.* Publications of the De Nobili Research Library, Vol. XVIII, Vienna.

———. 2001. 'The Interrupted Sacrifice and the Sanskrit Epics'. *Journal of Indian Philosophy* 29, pp. 169–86.

———. 2004. 'Nīlakaṇṭha's Instruments of War: Modern, Vernacular, Barbarous'. *Indian Economic and Social History Review* 41, pp. 365–85.

———. 2005. 'What Makes a Work Traditional? On the Success of Nīlakaṇṭha's Mahābhārata Commentary'. In F. Squarcini (ed.), *Boundaries, Dynamics and Construction of Traditions in South Asia*, pp. 225–52. Firenze University Press, Italy; Munshiram Manoharlal, New Delhi.

———. 2010. 'Nīlakaṇṭha's Mahābhārata'. www.india-seminar.com/2010/608/608_c_minkowski.htm.

Mitchiner, John E. 1982. *Traditions of the Seven Ṛṣis.* Motilal Banarsidass, Delhi.

Mithen, Steven. 2006. *The Singing Neanderthals.* Harvard University Press, Cambridge, MA.

Mitra, Anand. 1991. *Television and Popular Culture in India.* Sage, New Delhi.

Muellner, Leonard. 1996. *The Anger of Achilles: Mēnis in Greek Epic.* Cornell University Press, Ithaca, NY.

Nagy, Gregory. 1974. *Comparative Studies in Greek and Indic Meter.* Harvard Studies in Comparative Literature 33. Harvard University Press, Cambridge, MA.

———. 1979. *The Best of the Achaeans.* Johns Hopkins University Press, Baltimore, MD.

———. 1996a. *Poetry as Performance.* Cambridge University Press, Cambridge.

———. 1996b. *Homeric Questions.* University of Texas Press, Austin.

———. 2003. *Homeric Responses.* University of Texas Press, Austin.

———. 2006. 'The Epic Hero', 2nd ed. (online version). Center for Hellenic Studies, Washington, DC. Available at: https://chs.harvard.edu/CHS/article/display/1302.gregory-nagy-the-epic-hero (accessed 13 May 2019).

———. 2012. 'Signs of Hero Cult in Homeric Poetry'. In F. Montanari, A. Rengakos and C. Tsagalis (eds), *Homeric Contexts: Neoanalysis and the Interpretations of Homeric Poetry*, pp. 27–71. Trends in Classics Supplementary Vol. 12. Berlin and Boston.

———. 2013. *The Ancient Greek Hero in Twenty-Four Hours.* Harvard University Press, Cambridge, MA.

Nair, Karthika. 2015. *Until the Lions.* Arc Publications, Todmorden.

Nikam, N. A., and Richard McKeon. 1959. *The Edicts of Aśoka.* University of Chicago Press, Chicago, IL.

Ogden, C. K., and I. A. Richards. *The Meaning of Meaning.* Kegan Paul, Trench and Trubner, London.

Olivelle, Patrick. 1993. *The Āśrama System.* Oxford University Press, New York.

———. (ed.). 2004. 'Dharma: Studies in Its Semantic, Cultural, and Religious History'. *Journal of Indian Philosophy*, 32(5–6), special issue.

———. (ed.). 2006. *Between the Empires*. Oxford University Press, New York.

———. 2009. *Aśoka*. Motilal Banarsidass, Delhi.

———. 2011. *Ascetics and Brahmins*. Anthem Press, New York.

———. 2017. *A Dharma Reader*. Columbia University Press, New York.

Pache, Corinne. 2018. 'A Word from Another World'. *Classical Receptions Journal* 10(2), pp. 17–19.

Padoux, André. 1990. *Vāc: The Concept of the Word*. Translated by Jacques Gontier. State University of New York Press, Albany.

Pal, Pratapaditya. 1986. *Indian Sculpture*. Vol. I. Los Angeles County Museum of Art, University of California Press, Los Angeles.

Paṇḍita, Puruṣottama. 1953. *The Early Brahmanical System of Gotra and Pravara*. John Brough, trans. and introduction. Cambridge University Press, Cambridge.

Pargiter, F. E. 1908. 'The Nations of India at the Battle between the Pāṇḍavas and the Kauravas'. *Journal of the Royal Asiatic Society* 40(2), pp. 309–36.

——— (ed.). 1913. *The Purāna Text of Dynasties of the Kali Age*. H. Milford, London.

———. 1922. *The Ancient Indian Historical Tradition*. Oxford University Press, London.

Parke, H. W. 1977. *Festivals of the Athenians*. Cornell University Press, Ithaca, NY.

Parpola, Asko. 1994. *Deciphering the Indus Script*. Cambridge University Press, Cambridge.

———. 2002. 'Pandaiē and Sitā: On the Historical Background of the Sanskrit Epics'. *Journal of the American Oriental Society* 122, pp. 361–73.

———. 2004–5. 'The Nāsatyas, the Chariot, and Proto-Aryan Religion'. *Journal of Indological Studies* 16–17, pp. 1–63.

———. 2015. *The Origins of Hinduism*. Oxford University Press, New York.

Parry, M. 1932. 'Studies in the Epic Technique of Oral Versemaking: II. The Homeric Language as the Language of Oral Poetry'. *Harvard Studies in Classical Philology* 43, pp. 1–50.

Peabody, Norbert. 2003. *Hindu Kingship and Polity in Precolonial India*. Cambridge University Press, Cambridge.

Pfeiffer, Rudolph. 1968. *History of Classical Scholarship from the Beginnings to the End of the Hellenistic Age*. Oxford University Press, London.

Philostratus, Flavius. 2004. *The Hērōikos*. Edited and translated by Ellen Bradshaw Aitken and Jennifer Berenson Maclean. Society of Biblical Literature, Atlanta.

Pinch, William R. 2006. *Warrior Ascetics and Indian Empires*. Cambridge University Press, Cambridge.

Pontillo, Tiziana. 2016. 'Droṇa and Bhīṣma as Borderline Cases in Brāhmaṇical Systemization'. In I. Andrijanic and S. Sellmer (eds), *On the Growth and Composition of the Sanskrit Epics and Puranas: Proceedings of the Fifth Dubrovnik International Conference on the Sanskrit Epics and Puranas*, pp. 205–46. Croatian Academy of Sciences and Arts, Ibis Grafika, Zagreb.

Possehl, G. L. 2002. *The Indus Civilization*. AltaMira Press, Walnut Creek, CA.

Postans, Marianna. 1839. *Cutch; or, Random Sketches*. Smith, Elder, London.

Privitera, Siobhán Marie. 2015. 'Brain, Body, and World: Cognitive Approaches to the Iliad and Odyssey'. PhD dissertation, University of Edinburgh Archives.

Proclus. 1914. *Epic Cycle*. In Hugh G. Evelyn-White (ed. and trans.), *Hesiod, Homeric Hymns, Epic Cycle, Homerica*. Loeb Classical Library, Cambridge Mass.

Rapson, E. J. 1897. *Indian Coins*. K. J. Trübner, Strassburg.

Reddy, R. Chandrasekhara. 1994. *Heroes, Cults and Memorials: Andhra Pradesh, 300 A.D.–1600 A.D.* New Era Publications, Madras.

Rosand, Ellen, and Sergio Vartolo. 2007. Programme notes to *Il Ritorno d'Ulisse in Patria*, by Claudio Monteverdi. Brilliant Classics, Leeuwarden, Netherlands.

Roy, Kumkum, and Naina Dayal (eds). 2018. *Questioning Paradigms, Constructing Histories*: A *Festschrift for Romila Thapar*. Aleph Book Company, New Delhi.

Ryle, Gilbert. 1949. *The Concept of Mind*. Hutchinson's University Library, London.

Sahlins, Marshall. 2017. *Stone Age Economics*. Routledge Classics, New York.

Samuel, G. 2008. *The Origins of Yoga and Tantra*. Cambridge University Press, Cambridge.

Sappho. 1924. *Lyra Graeca*. Edited by J. M. Edmonds. Loeb Classical Library, Cambridge, MA.

Sarkar, Bihani. 2017. *Heroic Shāktism: The Cult of Durgā in Ancient Indian Kingship*. The British Academy, Oxford University Press, Oxford.

Sarmah, Thaneswar. 1991. *The Bharadvājas in Ancient India*. Motilal Banarsidass, Delhi.

Sathaye, Adheesh. 2010. 'The Other Kind of Brahman: Rāma Jāmadagnya and the Psychosocial Construction of Brahman Power in the Mahābhārata'. In S. Pollock (ed.), *Epic and Argument in Sanskrit Literary Theory: Essays in Honor of Robert P. Goldman*, pp. 185–207. Manohar, Delhi.

Satyamurti, Carole. 2015. *Mahabharata: A Modern Retelling*. Norton, New York.

Sax, William. 2002. *Dancing the Self*. Oxford University Press, New York.

Scheuer, Jacques. 1982. *Śiva Dans le Mahābhārata*. Paris. Repr., Darmstadt, 1957.

Schreiner, Peter (ed.). 1997. *Nārāyaṇīya Studien*. Harrassowitz, Wiesbaden.

Scott, William C. 2009. *The Artistry of the Homeric Simile*. Dartmouth College Press, Hanover.

Seaford, Richard. 2004. *Money and the Early Greek Mind*. Cambridge University Press, Cambridge.

Searle, J. R. 1969. *Speech Acts*. Cambridge University Press, Cambridge.

Sellmer, Sven. 2009. 'Towards a Semantics of the Mental in the Indian Epics'. In P. Koskikallio (ed.), *Parallels and Comparisons: Proceedings of the Fourth Dubrovnik International Conference on the Sanskrit Epics and Puranas*, pp. 181–91. Croatian Academy of Sciences and Arts, Ibis Grafika, Zagreb.

———. 2015. *Formulaic Diction and Versification in the Mahābhārata*. Wydawnictwo Naukowe UAM, Poznań.

Sen, Amartya. 2005. *The Argumentative Indian*. Penguin Books, Delhi.

———. 2009. *The Idea of Justice*. Allen Lane, Delhi.

Sen, Shekhar. 2017. *The Dharma of Moksha, the Way of Liberation*. Review of P. Bhattacharya, translation of the *Mokṣadharma Parvan* of the *Śanti Parvan*, Writers' Workshop, Kolkata, 2016. Available at: http://www.boloji.com/articles/49557/the-dharma-of-moksha (accessed 13 May 2019).

Settar S., and Gunther D. Sontheimer (eds).1982. *Memorial Stones: A Study of Their Origin, Significance and Variety*. Institute of Indian Art, New Delhi.

Shakespeare, William. 1988. *The Complete Works*. Edited by Stanley Wells and Gary Taylor. Oxford University Press, Oxford.

Shalom, Naama. 2017. *Re-ending the Mahābhārata*. State University of New York Press, Albany.

Sharma, Arvind (ed.). 1991. *Essays on the Mahābhārata*. Brill, Leiden.

Sharma, J. P. 1968. *Republics in Ancient India*. Brill, Leiden.

Sharma, Ram Karan. 1966. 'Elements of Oral Poetry in the Mahābhārata'. In *Proceedings and Transactions of the All-India Oriental Congress* 1961, 21:2(1), pp. 43–49, BORI, Poona.

Sharma, Tej Ram. 1989. *A Political History of the Imperial Guptas*. Concept Publishing, New Delhi.

von Simpson, G. 1990. 'Text Layers in the Mahābhārata'. In R. N. Dandekar (ed.), *The Mahābhārata Revisited*, pp. 37–60. Sahitya Akademi, New Delhi.

Singh, Upinder. 2017. *Political Violence in Ancient India*. Harvard University Press, Cambridge, MA.

Skjærvø, Prods Oktor. 1994. 'Hymnic Composition in the Avesta'. *Die Sprache* 36(2), pp. 199–243. Harrassowitz Verlag, Wiessbaden.

———. 1998. 'Eastern Iranian Epic Traditions I: Siyāvaš and Kunāla'. In Jay Jasanoff, H. Craig Melchert and Lisi Olivier (eds), *Mír Curad: Studies in Honour of Calvert Watkins*, pp. 645–58. Sonderdruck, Innsbruck.

———. 2000. 'Eastern Iranian Epic Traditions III: Zarathustra and Diomēdēs – an Indo-European Epic Warrior Type'. *Bulletin of the Asia Institute* 11, pp. 175–82.

———. 2011. *The Spirit of Zoroastrianism*. Yale University Press, New Haven, CT.

Smith, J. D. 1987. 'Formulaic Language in the Epics of India'. In B. Almqvist, S. Ó Catháin and P. Ó Héalaí (eds), *The Heroic Process: Form, Function, and Fantasy in Folk Epic*, pp. 591–611. Glendale Press, Dublin.

———. 1991. *The Epic of Pābūjī*. Cambridge University Press, Cambridge.

Smith, M. C. 1975. 'The Mahābhārata's Core'. *Journal of the American Oriental Society* 95(3), pp. 479–82.

———. 1992. *The Warrior Code of India's Sacred Song*. Garland, New York.

Snell, Bruno. 1946. *Die Entdeckung des Geistes*. Claaszen & Goverts, Hamburg. 1953, T. G. Rosenmeyer (trans.), *The Discovery of the Mind*. Harvard University Press, Cambridge, MA.

Söhnen-Thieme, R. 2009. 'Buddhist Tales in the *Mahābhārata*?'. In P. Koskikallio (ed.), *Parallels and Comparisons: Proceedings of the Fourth Dubrovnik International Conference on the Sanskrit Epics and Puranas*, pp. 349–72. Croatian Academy of Sciences and Arts, Ibis Grafika, Zagreb.

Sörensen, S. 1904. *An Index to the Names in the Mahābhārata*. Copenhagen. Repr., Motilal Banarsidass, Delhi, 1978.

Sounes, Howard. 2001. *Down the Highway: The Life of Bob Dylan*. Doubleday, London. Revised, Grove Press, New York, 2011.

Southworth, Franklin. 2005. *Linguistic Archaeology of South Asia*. Routledge, London.

Stone, Keith A. 2016. *Singing Moses' Song*. Ilex Foundation, Harvard University Press, Cambridge, MA.

Sukthankar, Vishnu S. 1944. *Critical Studies in the Mahābhārata*. Karnatak Publishing House, Bombay.

———. 1957. *On the Meaning of the Mahābhārata*. Asiatic Society of Bombay.

Sullivan, Bruce M. 1999. *Seer of the Fifth Veda*. Motilal Banarsidass, Delhi.

Száler, Péter. 2018. 'Who Was Śalya's Father?'. *Asiatische Studien* 73(1).

Tarrant, R. J. 2016. *Texts, Editors, and Readers*. Cambridge University Press, Cambridge.

Thakur, Anatalal. 2015. 'Mahabharatjuddhe Duiti Truti'. In *Nibandhabali*, pp. 160–61, New Age Publishers, Kolkata.

Thakuria, Tilok. 2011. 'Memorial Stones at Kanmer, Gujarat, India'. In Toshiki Osada (ed.), *Linguistics, Archaeology and Human Past*, pp. 175–87. Indus Project Research Institute for Humanity and Nature, Kyoto.

Thapar, Romila. 1978. *Ancient Indian Social History*. Orient Longman, New Delhi.

———. 1992. *Interpreting Early India*. Oxford University Press, New Delhi.

———. 1996. *Time as a Metaphor of History*. Oxford University Press, New Delhi.

———. 2002. *Early India*. Penguin Press, Delhi.

———. 2013. *The Past before Us*. Permanent Black, Orient Black Swan, Delhi.

Thapar, Valmik, Romila Thapar and Yusuf Ansari. 2013. *Exotic Aliens*. Aleph Book Company, New Delhi.

Tharoor, S. 1989. *The Great Indian Novel*. Penguin Books, New Delhi.

Thomas, Richard F. 2007. 'The Streets of Rome: The Classical Dylan'. *Oral Tradition* 22(1), pp. 30–56.

———. 2017a. *Why Bob Dylan Matters*. HarperCollins, New York.

———. 2017b. 'The Metamorphosis of Dylan'. *Times Literary Supplement*, 6 December.

Thompson, G. 1997. 'On Truth-Acts in Vedic'. *Indo-Iranian Journal* 41, pp. 125–53.

Tieken, Herman. 2004. 'The Mahābhārata after the Great Battle'. *Wiener Zeitschrift für die Kinde Südasiens* 48, pp. 5–46.

Tolkien, J. R. R. 1954–55. *The Lord of the Rings*. 3 vols. Allen and Unwin, London.

Tomlinson, Gary. 2015. *A Million Years of Music*. Zone Books, New York.

Trautmann, T. R. 1974. 'Cross-Cousin Marriage in Ancient North India?'. In T. R. Trautmann (ed.), *Kinship and History in South Asia*, pp. 61–103. University of Michigan, Ann Arbor.

———. 1981. *Dravidian Kinship*. Cambridge University Press, Cambridge.

———. 2000. 'India and the Study of Kinship "Terminologies"'. *L'Homme* 154–55, pp. 559–72.

Tsagalis, Christos. 2012. *From Listeners to Viewers: Space in the Iliad*. Center for Hellenic Studies, Washington, DC.

Tsoukalas, S., and Gerald Surya (eds). 2015. *Studies in the Bhagavad Gita: Ontology*. Edwin Mellen Press, Lewiston, NY.

Tsuchida, Ryutaro. 2008. 'Considerations on the Narrative Structure of the Mahābhārata'. *Studies in Indian Philosophy and Buddhism* 15, pp. 1–26.

———. 2009. 'Some Reflections on the Chronological Problems of the Mahābhārata'. *Studies in Indian Philosophy and Buddhism* 16, pp. 1–24.

Tuck, A. 2006. 'Singing the Rug: Patterned Textiles and the Origins of Indo-European Metrical Poetry'. *American Journal of Archaeology* 110, pp. 539–50.

Turner, James. 2014. *Philology*. Princeton University Press, Princeton, NJ.

Vassilkov, Yaroslav. 1995. 'The Mahābhārata's Typological Definition Considered'. *Indo-Iranian Journal* 38, pp. 249–56.

———. 2016. 'The Mahābhārata and Non-Vedic Aryan Traditions'. In I. Andrijanic and S. Sellmer (eds), *On the Growth and Composition of the Sanskrit Epics and Puranas: Proceedings of the Fifth Dubrovnik International Conference on the Sanskrit Epics and Puranas*, pp. 181–203. Croatian Academy of Sciences and Arts, Ibis Grafika, Zagreb.

Verardi, Giovanni. 2011. *Hardships and Downfall of Buddhism in India*. Manohar, Delhi.

Vielle, Christophe. 1996. *Le Mytho-Cycle Héroique dans l'Aire Indo-Européene*. Institute Orientaliste, Louvain-la-Neuve.

Watkins, Calvert. 1985. *The American Heritage Dictionary of Indo-European Roots*. Houghton Mifflin, Boston.

———. 1995. *How to Kill a Dragon: Aspects of Indo-European Poetics*. Oxford University Press, Oxford.

Weil, Simone. 1948. *La Pesanteur et la Grâce*. Plon, Paris.

West, M. L. 2007. *Indo-European Poetry and Myth*. Oxford University Press, Oxford.

Wheeler, R. E. M. 1968. *The Indus Civilisation*. 3rd ed. Cambridge University Press, Cambridge.

Whicher, Ian, and David Carpenter (eds). 2003. *Yoga: The Indian Tradition.* RoutledgeCurzon, London.

Williams, Raymond Brady. 2001. *An Introduction to Swaminarayan Hinduism.* Cambridge University Press, Cambridge.

Wiser, William Henricks. 1936. *The Hindu Jajmani System.* Lucknow Publishing House, Lucknow.

Witzel, E. J. Michael. 1997. 'Early Sanskritization. Origins and Development of the Kuru State'. In B. Kölver, *Staat und Recht im Klassischen Indien.* Oldenbourg, Munchen.

———. 2012. *The Origins of the World's Mythologies.* Oxford University Press, New York.

Woodard, Roger D. 2008. *Indo-European Sacred Space.* University of Illinois Press, Urbana.

———. 2013. *Myth, Ritual, and the Warrior in Roman and Indo-European Antiquity.* Cambridge University Press, New York.

———. 2014. *The Textualization of the Greek Alphabet.* Cambridge University Press, Cambridge.

Xenophon. 1922. *Anabasis.* Translated by Carleton L. Brownson. Revised by John Dillery, 1998, 2001. Loeb Classical Library, Cambridge, MA.

Yalman, Nur. 1967. *Under the Bo Tree: Studies in Caste, Kinship, and Marriage in the Interior of Ceylon.* University of California Press, Berkeley.

———. 1969. 'De Tocqueville in India: An Essay on the Caste System'. *Man,* New Series, 4(1), March, pp. 123–31.

Yoffee, R. 2005. *Myths of the Archaic State.* Cambridge University Press, Cambridge.

Zanker, Andreas T. 2019. *Metaphor in Homer: Time, Speech, and Thought.* Cambridge University Press, Cambridge [forthcoming].

Zunshine, L. 2006. *Why We Read Fiction: Theory of Mind and the Novel.* Ohio State University Press, Columbus.

INDEX

Abhimanyu 16, 45, 50, 62
abhiṣeka 54
adharma 36, 36n49, 37
Ādi *parvan* 6, 8, 29, 40, 45, 47, 71, 76, 79, 80, 81
Amartya Sen ix, 35, 36
Anugītā 66
Anuśāsana *parvan* 29
aoidos 9, 10
Appendix on Epic Achilles 104n31
Appendix on Epic Preliteracy 5n8
Appendix on Epic Time 28n25
Āraṇyaka *parvan* 51, 53n11
Arjuna ii, 13, 14, 15, 16, 24, 41, 45, 50, 52n9, 53, 54, 55, 57, 59, 61, 62, 66, 67, 68, 68n26, 69, 74, 105, 109, 111
Āryan 3, 24, 25, 41, 42, 55, 80, 82, 84
aśvamedha 32, 52
Āśvamedhika *parvan* 65
Aśvatthāman 61

Bachvarova 23, 23n10, 23n11, 41n59, 105
bhāratavarṣa 28, 35
Bhārgava Recension 16, 73
bheda 15, 30, 31n30, 48, 74, 76
Bhīṣma ii, 2, 4, 10, 11, 12, 13, 13n10, 14, 15, 16, 17, 19, 21, 28n24, 30, 31, 31n30, 34, 36, 39, 41, 54, 55, 59, 60, 64, 65, 76, 76n4, 111, 113
Bhṛgu 2n3, 16, 73
Bombay Edition 1n1, 8n4, 40n58, 61n18
brāhmaṇa 30, 56, 66, 81
bricolage 29, 75

chariot 27n22, 57
Chariot Song 14, 27, 59, 66

daivam 62
Dhārtarāṣṭra 6, 16, 17, 30, 74
Dhṛtarāṣṭra 30, 47, 49, 53n11, 57, 58, 59, 62, 63, 66, 67, 71, 72, 76
dhyāna 7, 10, 11, 13, 15, 17, 18, 23n8, 110
divyaṃ cakṣur 9, 13, 54
Draupadī 27, 35, 41, 48, 52, 52n9, 57, 61, 69, 74, 76, 98n21, 108
Droṇa 13, 13n10, 27, 60, 113
Dumézil 33n36, 107, 108
Duryodhana 15, 24, 49, 54, 71, 74, 75n3, 108, 110
dyarchy 32, 33n36

Gāndhārī 24, 47, 49, 63, 63n20, 66, 67
Gaṅgā 65, 66
Gītā 13, 59, 66, 111
Guru Pūrṇimā 83

Hāstinapura 12, 14, 16, 28n24, 30, 33, 45, 53n11, 57, 64, 72, 74, 76
Hinduism 25, 41, 73, 113, 117
Homeric Question 8

Indo-Āryan 13, 30, 30n28
Indraprastha 16, 28n24, 30, 33, 52
Indus Valley Civilization 26

Janamejaya 8, 29, 30, 45, 46, 48, 50, 55, 56, 67, 71, 72, 73, 74, 75, 76, 90
Jaya ii, 7, 8, 8n4, 10, 11, 18, 19, 47, 48, 50, 59, 111

Kali Yuga 57
Karṇa 15, 21, 24, 31, 32, 35, 36, 38, 39, 41, 54, 59n17, 60, 76, 111
kīrti 6, 31, 32, 37

Kṛṣṇa ii, 1, 5, 11, 12, 13, 13n10, 14, 15, 15n12, 16, 17, 19, 21, 27, 30n29, 32, 33, 35, 36, 41, 45, 46, 49, 50, 52n9, 55, 57, 59, 60, 62, 65, 66, 68, 69, 73, 74, 76, 79, 82, 106, 108, 111
Kuntī 15, 30, 35, 47, 51, 52, 60, 74
Kuru 16, 24, 25n16, 30, 47, 117
Kurukṣetra Books 4, 9, 10, 22, 25n17, 29, 33n35, 38, 54, 58, 87

lex talionis 37, 100

Mānava *dharmaśāstra* 2n3, 16, 36
matriline 16, 30, 45
Matrilineal 30
Mausala 25n17
metaphor 3, 4, 6, 10, 28, 29, 32, 36, 39, 68, 69, 72, 72n1, 91, 98n21, 100n25
metonymy 2, 6, 29, 56, 85, 96n14, 100n25
money 27, 33, 35, 37

Nagy ix, 4, 5, 5n13, 9, 9n6, 21n1, 87n1, 111, 112
Naimiṣa 46, 47, 56, 67, 71, 72, 73, 81
Nārada 11, 27, 54, 55n13, 61, 62, 88n5
Nārāyaṇa 60, 73
Nīlakaṇṭha 1n1

Pāṇḍu 47, 49, 74, 76
Paraśurāma 17, 24, 28n24, 30, 57n16
Pargiter 23, 24n12, 24n13, 24n15, 26, 113
Parikṣit 16, 30, 50, 57, 67
parvasaṃgraha 9, 47n4, 57, 72
plot 4, 5, 5n15, 6, 7, 13, 15, 16, 17, 18, 19, 24, 29, 35, 37, 40, 49, 51, 53, 53n11, 54, 56, 57, 58, 61n18, 62, 65, 65n23, 66, 68, 69, 72, 73, 74, 75, 76, 77, 80, 81, 84, 88, 90, 92, 92n8, 93n10, 94, 95, 96, 98n21, 100, 101, 102, 103, 104
polytropic 3, 28, 47, 51, 82, 87, 99, 101
preliteracy 2, 27, 33
premonetary 2n4, 27, 36, 84, 85, 90
pūjā 27
Pūru 31, 76

rāja Yudhiṣṭhira 12, 15, 15n12, 16, 24, 34, 53n11, 55, 60, 61, 64, 65, 66, 66n25
rājasūya 15, 16, 32, 48, 52, 54, 56, 57, 64, 65, 74, 76, 82, 98n21
Rāma 17, 27, 102n29, 106, 114
rhapsōidos 9, 10
Ring composition 46n3
Rudra-Śiva 2, 60

sabhā 12, 13, 14, 31, 35, 62
Sabhā *parvan* 55, 57, 98n21
Śakuntalā 35, 76
Śalya *parvan* 60
Saṃjaya 1, 2, 4, 9, 9n7, 10, 13, 18, 23n8, 28, 38, 51, 53n11, 54, 55, 57, 58, 59, 60, 61, 62, 63, 67, 71, 72, 75
Śaṃtanu 29, 76
Samudragupta 17n15, 26
Śānti *parvan* 14, 15, 29, 64
śastrayajña 32
Satyavatī 30, 45, 46, 49, 50, 71, 74, 75, 76, 82
Śaunaka 16, 71, 73, 74
Sauptika *parvan* 25n17, 61, 61n18
Shakespeare 4, 22n6, 33n37, 42n62, 54n12, 110, 114
Shield of Achilles 37
Śikhaṇḍin 15
simile 29, 39, 89
Smith, M. C. 17, 17n16
speech act 8, 51, 51n7, 58, 62, 90, 92, 92n8, 93, 94, 95, 96, 96n15, 97, 99, 101n27, 103, 103n30, 104
story 5, 5n15, 6, 16, 17, 18, 19, 21n3, 24, 29, 40, 57, 65n23, 66, 72, 75, 76, 81, 83, 88, 90, 94, 96, 97n18, 98n21, 101, 102
Śuka 46n2, 65, 65n23, 81
Sukthankar 16, 18, 73, 108, 115
Svargārohaṇa *parvan* 40
svayaṃvaras 35

Takṣaśilā 8, 10, 23, 46, 73, 90
Tharoor 42, 42n60, 82, 82n3, 105, 115
the Bhārata 6, 8, 8n3, 8n4, 10, 11, 16, 19, 24, 26, 29, 33n35, 35, 40, 47, 47n4, 48, 50, 51, 53n10, 65, 67, 72, 73, 74, 81
theophany 12, 13, 13n10, 14

Ugraśravas 2, 2n3, 16, 28, 45, 46, 48, 55, 56, 60, 67, 71, 72, 73, 74, 75, 76, 81
Upaplavya 24n15

ur-Bhārata 17
Uttarā 57, 62

Vaiśaṃpāyana 1, 2n3, 9, 10, 28, 45, 46, 47, 48, 52, 53n10, 55, 56, 60, 65, 66, 67, 71, 73, 74, 75, 75n3, 76, 81
vendetta 37, 37n52, 100
Vidura 13, 13n10, 47, 49, 55, 62
Virāṭa *parvan* 57
Virgil 22n6, 54n12
Vyāsa's Bhārata 9, 19, 73

Watkins 23n10, 31n31, 115, 116

Yādava 16, 24, 29, 30, 30n27, 46, 50, 62, 82
Yadu 31, 76
Yayāti 31, 76
yugas 28

www.ingramcontent.com/pod-product-compliance
Lightning Source LLC
Chambersburg PA
CBHW021834300426
44114CB00009BA/432
* 9 7 8 1 7 8 5 2 7 5 7 4 6 *